W9-BSQ-066

FRAME-LOOM WEAVING

JANE REDMAN

VAN NOSTRAND REINHOLD COMPANY
New York Cincinnati Toronto London Melbourne

Dedicated To My Teacher
Else Regensteiner

Copyright © 1976 by Litton Educational Publsihing, Inc.
Library of Congress Catalog Card Number 75-20693
ISBN 0-442-26860-2

All rights reserved. No part of this work covered by the copyright
hereon may be reproduced or used in any form or by any means—
graphic, electronic, or mechanical, including photocopying, record-
ing, taping, or information storage and retrieval systems—without
written permission of the publisher.
Printed in the United States of America
Designed by Loudan Enterprises

Published in 1976 by Van Nostrand Reinhold Company
A Division of Litton Educational Publishing, Inc.
450 West 33rd Street
New York, NY 10001

Van Nostrand Reinhold Limited
1410 Birchmount Road
Scarborough, Ontario M1P 2E7, Canada

Van Nostrand Reinhold Australia Pty. Ltd.
17 Queen Street
Mitcham, Victoria 3132, Australia

Van Nostrand Reinhold Company Ltd.
Molly Millars Lane
Wokingham, Berkshire, England

16 15 14 13 12 11 10 9 8 7 6 5 4 3 2 1

Library of Congress Cataloging in Publication Data

Redman, Jane.
  Frame-loom weaving.

  Bibliography: p.
  Includes index.
  1. Hand weaving. 2. Looms. I. Title.
TT848.R35   746.1′4   75-20693
ISBN 0-442-26860-2

ACKNOWLEDGMENTS

This book is the culmination of many ideas that have evolved in several years of teaching frame-loom weaving. I am indebted to the authors included in the bibliography and to the many inventive and creative people who have opened up a wealth of new directions in preparing foundations for individual expression and exploration.

Many thanks to Hector Garcia and to Robert Fields for their photographs. I would also like to express my gratitude to Robert Gregson, for his excellent drawings; to Kathy Tenner, who helped complete the illustrations; and to Evelyn Pope, for typing the manuscript.

Thanks to Gwynne Lott, Sharon Shattan, Suzanne Gaston-Voute, Joanna Staniskis, and Patricia Warner for their examples and help in contacting other weavers who use a frame loom.

Sincere thanks to Christa Mayer-Thurman for the use of the Textile Study Room and the photographs from the collection of the Art Institute of Chicago. And thanks to Adele Siegel of Arras Gallery for her help.

The book would never have been started or finished without the encouragement and insight of my editors, Nancy Newman Green and Wendy Lochner.

I am also grateful for the patience of my family, mother, and friends.

CONTENTS

Frontispiece. Jane Redman. Detail of a wall
hanging. See figure 2–10.

INTRODUCTION

This book is written for everyone who is concerned with weaving as a means of expression and a visual communication of an idea. It is intended for people who are interested in exploring the potential and characteristics of the woven object, who are excited by the touch of fibers, and who find pleasure in creating images.

The emphasis is on the construction and use of simple, inexpensive equipment to produce well-made, personally satisfying designs. A wide range of techniques and approaches is included to demonstrate the adaptability of the frame loom and the many ways in which the elements of design can be organized to form an infinite number of possibilities.

Weaving combines the sensation of seeing and perceiving with the sensation of touch. The creative weaver must become conscious of how concepts and visions in the imagination can be translated into a structured reality that is seen as well as felt. This awareness comes through an understanding of the relationships between design, technique, fiber, form, and function.

I-1. A frame loom is portable, adaptable, and inexpensive. Here, children are weaving on individual frame looms in a class at Fibre and Form. (Photo: Robert Fields)

Whether it is done for utilitarian, decorative, artistic, or a combination of purposes, weaving has always been a fascinating and compelling process for many people in different cultures, countries, and times.

It is an integral part of civilization, and the articles that have been produced are a reflection and an indication of the diverse lifestyles that have existed throughout history.

In our own era of sophisticated technology where we are able to use machines to manufacture mass materials with great speed and ease, there also exists the desire to make or seek out the unique, the one-of-a-kind, as an assertion of our own in-dividuality.

A book of this nature tends to skim lightly over the surface, and each chapter could easily be a book in itself. My hope is that it may be a starting point for those who are interested in the techniques and the craft of weaving as well as a catalyst for weavers who are trying to develop and strengthen their design potential.

I-2. Patricia Warner. Wall hanging in tapestry weave (detail). (Photo: Hector Garcia)

CHAPTER 1.

LOOMS

A DEFINITION OF WEAVING

The weaving process is simple and versatile. To weave is to interlace flexible materials together at right angles to form a pliable surface—a fabric, a cloth, or what is sometimes called a *web*. One series of mobile, horizontal, crosswise threads—the *weft*, or *filling*—passes between another series of taut, vertical, lengthwise threads—the *warp*. The order in which the warp and weft pass over and under each other is the major factor involved in determining the weave and the physical structure of the final piece.

This basic principle evolved in a preceramic age. Yet the concept has such great potential that it has constantly been developed in new ways during the many thousands of years in which it has been applied to functional uses, aesthetic needs, and individual interpretations.

Weaving is done on a loom. The success of a design does not depend on the loom, however, but rather on the awareness, imagination, and intuition that the person who is creating possesses. The innovations in equipment that have been developed were designed to save time and increase efficiency.

1-1. Odette Brabec. Sampler of techniques, including tapestry weave, pile weaves, Egyptian knots, lace weaves, and double weave. (Photo: Hector Garcia)

1-2. Deanette Murdough. Sampler of techniques, including macramé on the warp threads, wrapping, pile weaves, and tapestry weave. (Photo: Hector Garcia)

1-3. Edwina Beier. Wall hanging in tapestry weave. (Photo: Hector Garcia)

1-4. Joyce Richards. Wall hanging in double weave. The piece is framed with a stuffed tubular double weave and incorporates wrapping into the design. (Photo: Robert Fields)

1-5. *The City*. Joan Soderberg. Wall hanging in two layers: the bottom layer is tapestry weave; the top layer, Ghiordes knots with cut and uncut loops. The top layer uses tapestry checks, columns, and grids to suggest buildings. (Courtesy of Bonnie Kondor; photo: Hector Garcia)

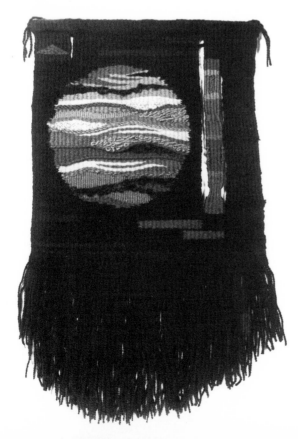

A DEFINITION OF THE LOOM

The loom is the weaver's most important tool. Whether it is complex or simple, one of the major functions of a loom is to keep the warp threads in order and under tension. The parts of different kinds of looms vary in appearance, but they serve the same purpose. Every loom has some method of raising and lowering selected combinations of warp threads. When some warp threads are raised while others remain stationary, what is known as a *shed* is created. A shed is an opening in the warp, a triangular space formed between warp threads through which horizontal threads pass and are laid, or *beaten*, into place. By passing the weft back and forth between alternate sheds the threads are interlocked and bound together. The weave, the construction, the technique, the stitches, and the knots remain the same. Once a technique is mastered and understood, it can usually be adapted and transferred from one project to another regardless of the type of loom that is used. Even elaborate weaving can be done on a simple loom. It is only a question of time and size.

The industrial power loom, the handloom, the tapestry loom, and the frame loom all have certain characteristics in common and follow the same fundamental weaving processes. The main differences are the speed with which something is woven and the possible combinations of form, shape, yarn, thread manipulation, and organization. The selection of a loom for weaving depends on the purpose of the project. The weaver must decide if a particular loom supplies a mechanical advantage or a mechanical restriction to the execution of an idea.

Designs that are based on repetition of the same pattern unit are best worked on a handloom, which gives speed and precision to what would otherwise become a tedious and monotonous task. The frame loom is more suitable to projects that require time for thought, flexibility, changes, decisions, and exploration of form and shape.

A consideration of the mechanics involved in weaving will explain the relationship of the frame loom to the handloom.

THE JACK-TYPE HANDLOOM

A *jack-type handloom* has thirteen main parts (if it is a floor loom): warp beam, back beam, heddles, harnesses, beater, reed, dents, front beam, apron, cloth beam, ratchets, treadles, and lams. Each part fulfills a special function either in maintaining even tension, spacing the warp threads, or forming the sheds.

1. The *warp beam* is a roller which holds the warp threads; they unwind from the beam as the weaving progresses. The roller system allows the length of the weaving to be much longer than the length of the loom, or what is sometimes referred to as an *infinite warp.*

2. The *back beam* is the beam over which the warp threads pass from the warp beam to the heddles.

3. The *heddles* are made from wire or string, and each one has an opening—an eye in the center—through which each individual warp thread passes. The heddles separate the warp threads from each other.

4. The *harnesses* raise and lower the warp threads. A loom may have two, four, six, eight, or more harnesses. Each harness is composed of two horizontal heddle bars attached at both top and bottom of an open heddle frame. The heddles are hung between the two bars.

5. The *beater* is attached to the loom framework, and it swings against the weft to position it evenly and horizontally.

6. The *reed* is a comblike device, made of either metal or wood. It is placed inside the beater and spreads the warp threads. Reeds come in different sizes and are interchangeable. They are classified by number of openings, or dents, per inch: a number 12 reed has twelve dents to an inch.

7. The *dents* are the open spaces in the reed that keep the warp threads in order and determine how close together they are.

8. The *front beam* is the beam over which the warp threads pass from the reed to the cloth beam.

9. The *apron* is a piece of fabric or a series of tapes nailed to the cloth beam and to the warp beam. The warp is tied to the *apron stick.*

10. The *cloth beam* is a roller on which the woven fabric is wound.

11. The *ratchets* are attached to both the cloth beam and the warp beam. They are either metal or wooden wheels with cogs—teeth into which a pawl, or tongue, falls. They are used to alternately release the warp and tighten it again as the completed weaving is wound onto the cloth beam and more warp unwinds from the warp beam.

12. The *treadles* on a floor loom are operated by the feet. They are pressed down by the feet according to the sequence of the weave.

13. The *lams* are short, horizontal sticks above the treadles and under each harness. Each lam is attached to both the harness above and the treadle below by either chains or ropes.

The warp on a handloom is handled in this manner (figure 1-6): the warp threads unwind from the warp beam under an equal tension and parallel to each other, pass over the back beam, through the heddles in the harnesses to the beater, through the dents in the reed, and over the front beam, where they are tied onto the apron stick and wound onto the cloth beam as the fabric is woven. Before the warp is put on the handloom, the threads must be measured, counted, and precut.

When the foot presses down on a treadle, it changes the horizontal position of the lams. The lams in turn push the harness up, and the heddles automatically lift the warp threads (figure 1-7). Each warp thread passes through only one heddle, and the warp threads are distributed individually in the harnesses. When a harness is raised, all the warp threads in that particular harness will be raised at the same time. When one set of warp threads is raised, the remaining threads stay stationary, thus creating a triangular opening in the warp, a shed, for the weft to pass through. When the treadle is released by the foot, the harness is lowered. A different shed is formed by pressing down on another treadle and raising another set of warp threads.

1-6. The warp on a handloom is handled in this manner: the warp threads unwind from the warp beam (1), pass over the back beam (2), through the heddles (3) in the harnesses (4) to the beater (5), through the dents (7) in the reed (6), and over the front beam (8), where they are tied onto the apron (9), wound onto the cloth beam (10), and alternately tightened and loosened by the ratchets (11) as the fabric, or web, is woven.

1-7. When the foot presses down on a treadle (12), the horizontal position of the lams (13) is changed and the harness is pushed up, causing all the threads in that particular harness to be lifted automatically.

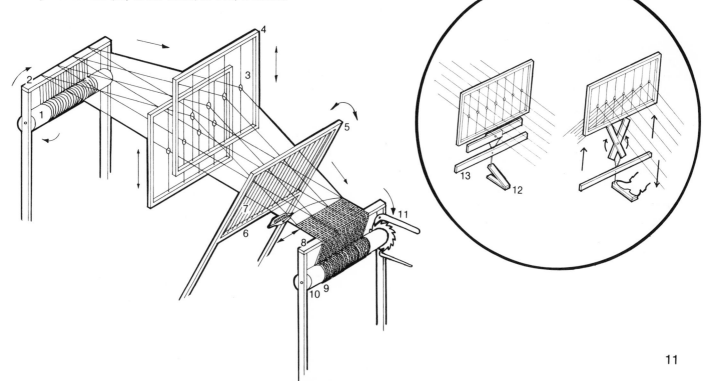

The weft is inserted from one edge to the other—from *selvage* to *selvage*—with a *shuttle*. Some shuttles, called *flat shuttles*, are made of sticks grooved at both ends to hold the yarn. The lengths of yarn are wound on and off by hand. Another method is to wind longer lengths of weft into *bobbins*, which are inserted into smooth, boatlike shuttles that slide easily across the bottom threads in the shed.

Although the reed, beater, cloth and warp beams, heddles, and harnesses save time and add to the efficiency of the weaving, they also present a few minor limitations. Not all fibers and yarns can be used for the warp. The yarn must be able to pass through the eye of the heddle, and it cannot be strung with any objects that cannot pass through the reed or be wound onto the beam. Fragile materials, bulky objects, glass, metal, shells, wood, or anything else that cannot bend or would be damaged if crushed can, however, be used on a nail frame loom, since the warp is stretched out flat.

The beater is effective for designs that develop in rows of weft that cross from side to side, but not all designs are horizontal. In some techniques such as slit tapestry some shapes and areas are developed before others and built up in a vertical direction (figure 1-8).

The cloth and warp beams are also limited to certain combinations of materials and techniques. An even tension must be maintained on the warp threads all the way across the warp. If one area is consistently built up in a heavy yarn or a dense technique, the warp will be taken up more and begin to tighten. It is easier to feel, see, and control the tightness and slackness of the warp in irregular weaves on a frame loom. A loom that allows the entire warp to be seen is best for planning and designing weaves in which the colors, shapes, and textures change and it is important to be able to relate the new parts to what has already been woven. Cloth that has been wound onto a beam must be unrolled if you want to view the work, and this will create a slight distortion in the way the parts of the design appear in relation to each other. The main considerations are the purpose of the weaving and the requirements of the project. Different looms will be appropriate for different kinds of weaving.

THE FRAME LOOM

Easy to assemble, portable, inexpensive, and adaptable, the frame loom is valuable for experimentation, for planning projects, as a teaching aid, or for making finished articles. It allows a wide variety of techniques, weaves, stitches, and knots that range from tapestry, double cloth, lace, and finger-manipulated weaves to twining and pile constructions such as rya. It permits many design possibilities that would not be practical on a more complex loom (see figures 1-1 through 1-5). A frame loom can be used to make purses, belts, clothing, rugs, and other functional items as well as wall hangings and pillows.

An excellent introduction to the vocabulary and concepts of weaving, the frame loom allows the beginner to develop a feeling for the materials used and to become acquainted with the interaction between fiber, form, and structure without purchasing a complicated and expensive loom. It is easier to decide what kind of loom to buy after you have been weaving for a while and know which is best suited to your own particular needs. More advanced weavers with many projects and ideas to test often

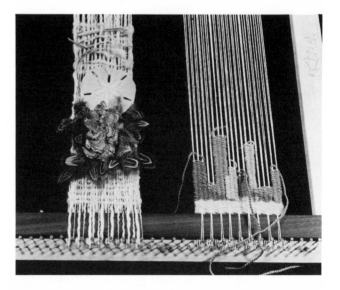

1-8. Tapestry does not have to be developed in rows of weft crossing from selvage to selvage: one shape may be formed before another is started. Bulky, fragile materials and highly textured warps may be used. (Photo: Hector Garcia)

find the frame loom ideal as an extra loom—or looms. It becomes a bit frustrating when ideas present themselves faster than you can finish a project. With several convenient frame looms it is not necessary to wait until the loom is empty before starting a new project. Ideas can be tested while they are still fresh and exciting. Projects left unfinished on the frame can be returned to as the design develops or when the incentive returns. The frame loom can be put to many purposes and leaves other looms free for weaving that requires mechanical control, speed, and efficiency.

If a class or a study group has a minimal amount of equipment, a limited budget, or a small working area, the frame loom becomes an asset and a marvelous teaching aid (figure 1-9). Enrollment does not have to be limited to the number of looms available, since the frame loom costs very little to make and requires only a small working or storage area. Money can be spent on yarn and materials rather than equipment. The frame loom can be worked on at a table or on the floor; it can be moved around the room or carried outside (figure 1-10).

1-10. The frame loom is very adaptable and requires little space. During a class, such as this one at Fibre and Form, students may work in groups of common interest and move around the room with the loom. The loom may be placed on a table, on the floor, or in any position that is comfortable for the weaver. (Photo: Robert Fields)

1-9. The author demonstrates the frame loom during a class at Fibre and Form. (Photo: Robert Fields)

The frame loom may even be the size of a wall, in which case the weaver works on a scaffold (figure 1-11). Students may work in groups or alone, and they can take the loom home for further study.

Two separate pieces can be woven on one frame loom at the same time (figure 1-12). One piece can be a sampler to explore different effects and perfect techniques, while the other piece can be a study of the visual relationships that structure a design. Used in this manner, the same loom can be applied to both class and individual problems. Combinations of colors, shapes, textures, weaves, yarns, and new materials can be tried and experimented with before attempting the final design. The designer is then able to anticipate the results before undertaking a total commitment.

One of the greatest advantages of the simple frame loom is that it brings the weaver in direct contact with the development and creation of a well-designed piece. Working slowly allows time for thought, planning, innovation, spontaneity, introspection, viewing, and understanding what is taking place.

Although a frame loom may be circular (figure 1-13), it is usually an open rectangle or square with some mechanism to keep the warp threads under tension. With such minimal requirements there are many variations, both commercial and individual. A few of the examples presented in this book were done on a rigid-heddle loom.

A *rigid-heddle frame loom*, also called a *hole-and-slot loom*, is composed of a row of thin, flat slats

1-11. *Pacific Moth.* Joanna Staniszkis. Tapestry, waxed-linen warp, 12′ × 30′. A simple line drawing serves as a guideline to the weavers. (Photo: Andrzej J. Rumel)

spaced at equal distances from each other and held together in a board (figure 1-14). Each slat has a small hole, or eye, in the center. One set of warp threads, strung through the eyes, is stationary; the other set, strung in the adjoining spaces, is movable. This allows two sheds to be created by raising or lowering alternate threads in the spaces. When the rigid heddle is either raised or lowered past the midway position, the warp threads are pulled either up or down, forming two different sheds.

Two frame looms were used for most of the projects in this book; they were selected because of their simplicity and versatility. In both cases the warp is wound directly onto the loom without any preliminary planning, counting, precutting, or measuring.

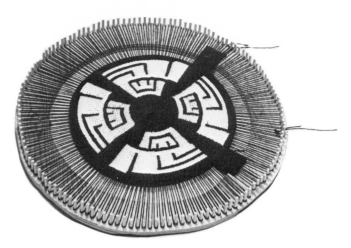

1-13. Stana Coleman. Woven piece on a circular frame loom. (Photo: Robert Fields)

1-12. The weaver may set up two separate warps on the frame loom and weave each one individually. One warp may be used for experiments and study in class, while the other warp may be woven at home or used for a specific project. (Photo: Paul Kondor)

1-14. A rigid-heddle frame loom is based on a hole-and-slot construction. Half of the warp threads remain stationary in the hole, while the other warp threads move up past the hole and then down below it, creating two alternate sheds through which the weft passes. The weft is usually wound on a flat shuttle with this type of loom. (Photo: Michael Ditlove, Inc.)

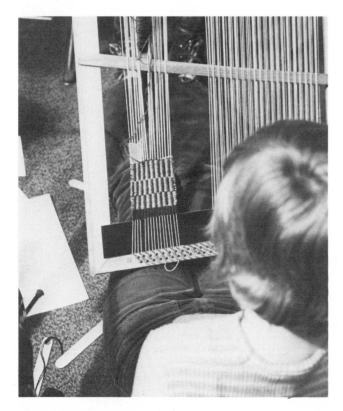

THE NAIL FRAME LOOM
Construction

The *nail frame loom*, the easiest to make, requires four canvas stretchers, two apiece of two different lengths, and two rows of nails on both the top and the bottom stretchers (figure 1-15).

Canvas stretchers are available at any art-supply store and come in a selection of sizes ranging from 8″ to 50″. The frame can be of any dimensions, but 16″ × 20″ or 18″ × 22″ are convenient sizes to start with and are comfortable to carry. Remember that the measurements *inside* the frame determine the length and width of the finished piece, not the outer measurements. Make sure that the stretchers are clean, straight, and without cracks. Test them at the store to see that the corners fit together securely and tightly.

Since they are based on the fin-and-slot principle (figure 1-16), the stretchers are easy to assemble and fit firmly together at right angles. If the corners seem wobbly, they can be reinforced with metal braces screwed down on the back of the frame. Wedges, or keys, are available with the stretchers and can also be used to secure the corners.

A picture frame can also be used if the sides are level, or a frame can be made from lumber. If you are using lumber, sandpaper all the rough edges. Attach the corners with wood screws long enough to pass through both thicknesses of wood where the sides overlap. Put washers under the screwheads and a binder head on the back of the frame. Keep the corners as close to right angles as possible (figure 1-17). Cover the screws with tape or some other protective covering if they protrude to keep them from scratching the furniture.

1-15. To construct a nail frame loom, you will need these materials: four canvas stretchers, nails, a pencil, a ruler, and a hammer. (Photo: Robert Fields)

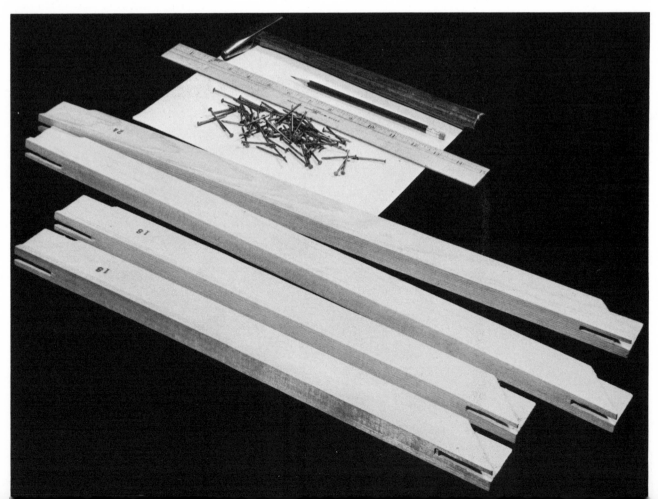

1-16. Fin-and-slot construction. The stretchers should fit securely together. Braces or metal angles should be screwed to the corners if the frame shifts around. (Photo: Robert Fields)

1-17. The frame should fit together at right angles as accurately as possible to ensure that the warp threads will be straight. (Photo: Robert Fields)

1-18. The two rows of nails should be hammered in firmly. (Photo: Robert Fields)

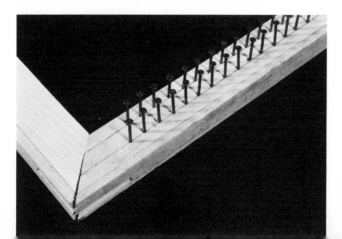

The size of the nails may vary. Nails that are 1 1/4" long work well. So do wire nails, which are not as heavy as other nails. It is important to hammer them firmly into the wood and to space them accurately (figure 1-18). Pine stretchers or any other soft wood are easy to hammer and saw through.

To estimate how many nails you need, multiply the number of nails per inch by the width of the space *inside* the frame. Count only the weaving width. For example, if you have 4 nails per inch and a 20" frame, you will need 80 nails for one side. Double that amount to include the top and bottom stretchers, and you will need a total of 160 nails. With a pencil and a ruler mark the placement of the nails (figure 1-19). Stagger the two rows; otherwise the wood might split. Start one row about 1" from the outside and 1/2" from the inside of the top and bottom stretchers. The nails should be 1/2" apart in each row, and the rows at least 1/4" apart. If the wood starts to crack, place the rows 1/2" apart. Start the second row 1/4" away from the starting point of the first row so that the first nail is in the middle of the first 2 nails in the previous row. The result is 4 nails per inch. To ensure that the warp threads will be straight, keep the nails in the top and bottom stretchers in line with each other.

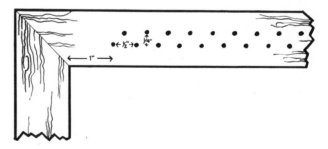

1-19. To space the nails, start at least 1" in from the inside of the side stretcher. The first row of nails starts 1/2" back from the inside of the top stretcher. The second row starts at least 1/4" to 1/2" behind the first row. The nails in each row should be 1/2" apart, but the second row should start 1/4" further in than the first row.

Warping

The number of warp threads per inch is called the *sett*. The sett must be flexible and adaptable to accommodate different techniques and different thicknesses of yarn and thread. A frame loom with 4 nails to the inch can be warped to have a sett of 4, 8, 12, or 16 threads to the inch, depending on the number of nails used and the order in which they are used when the warp is put on the loom.

For a sett of 4 threads to the inch use only one row of nails or every other nail. A sett of 8 threads to the inch is produced by using every nail (figure 1-20). For a sett of 12 threads to the inch two warps must be put on the same loom. Wind one warp on every nail for a sett of 8, then wind another warp on top of the first one, using one row of nails for a sett of 4 (figure 1-21). The two warps combined produce a sett of 12 threads per inch. For a sett of 16 wind two warps, each with a sett of 8, on the loom.

The warp on a nail frame is a finite warp, since it is limited by the length of the loom. Preparing the frame loom for weaving, or *dressing* the loom, is fast and uncomplicated. It does not matter whether the warp starts from the right or the left. Most people find it more comfortable to move from right to left. The starting nail does not have to be the last nail on the stretcher. If the piece requires a narrower weaving width, skip some nails and start further in towards the middle. The warp does not necessarily have to be centered on the loom; again, it depends on the width of the weaving.

The warp is wound directly onto the loom from the ball, spool, or cone of thread. Unwind a small portion of thread, enough to tie a clove-hitch knot (figure 1-22) or any other secure knot to the starting nail. Encircle the nail from right to left with the end of the thread, passing around the nail until the thread crosses over itself in front of the nail, forming a loop. Bring the end of the thread back to the left-hand side by passing it under the right-hand thread and then out over itself on the left side. Pull the loop tight and repeat the knot, again passing the left-hand thread over the right-hand thread, back under it, and out over itself on the left side. Pull the second knot tight to secure the first knot.

After the end is tied, the warp can be wound on the loom. Holding the warp in one hand, unroll it

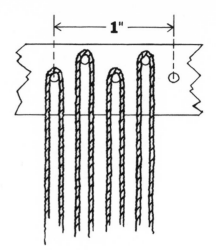

1-20. A sett of 8 threads, or warp ends, to the inch.

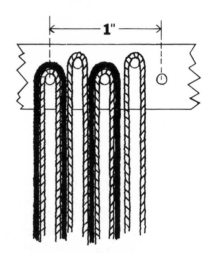

1-21. A sett of 12 threads to the inch.

1-22. A clove-hitch, or double-vertical-hitch, knot, used to tie the warp thread to the nail.

gradually. Wind the thread around the corresponding nail on the opposite stretcher, then around the next nail on the original stretcher. Continue winding the thread in this manner until the desired weaving width is warped (figure 1-23). End the thread with a clove-hitch knot on the same stretcher from which the warp started in order to maintain an even number of warp threads. The end threads on either side are the selvages. With a large project wind the first and the last warp threads twice around the same nail. This produces a double thread at each edge that reinforces the selvages.

Control of the tension is very important for a successful piece. Even tension is necessary for a woven piece to hang properly and to prevent unwanted buckling. Work towards absolute control over the tension and straight selvages. The warp threads should offer resistance, bounce back, and feel firm to the touch.

The warp is sometimes tighter on one side than the other, most often the side where it finishes, but this tension is adjustable. Starting from the tighter side and moving consecutively towards the slacker side, repeat the original path of the warp thread. Pull down away from the tight side of each nail and upward towards the slack side. Untie the end and knot it again on the last nail to take up the slack.

To estimate the amount of thread needed for the warp, multiply the number of threads per inch by the total width of the piece by the length of the warp. A warp with 8 threads per inch, a width of 18″, and a length of 20″, for example, requires 2880″, or 240′, of thread.

A frame with 4 nails to the inch is very versatile, especially for experiments and small samples. When it is warped on every nail, there are 8 threads to the inch. They can be woven in pairs and used as a sett of 4 threads to the inch or divided into two different warps and woven as separate top and bottom layers. This arrangement is adaptable to many weaves and techniques, such as tapestry, wrapping, knotting, looping, pile weaves, fringe techniques, finger-manipulated weaves, twining, double weaves, tubular weaves, plaids, and open, lacy effects, all of which are discussed in succeeding chapters.

1-23. Warping the nail frame loom. If a knot or flaw occurs in the warp thread, stop warping and return to the previous nail. Cut the flaw out and tie the warp to that nail. Start again by tying the warp to the next nail in sequence. Never leave a flaw in the warp: it may weaken or break, distort the weaving, or appear as a mistake. (Photo: Robert Fields)

Weaving

There are three basic weaves, or constructions of thread interlacement, that are not derived from any other system: *plain weave*, *twill weave*, and *satin weave*. Of the three plain weave is the most suited to the frame loom and the easiest to manipulate without the use of multiple harnesses. The sequence of the other two constructions is too complicated to follow without mechanical means. Plain, or tabby, weave is also the most basic and the strongest of all the woven constructions. It is the foundation for the majority of fabrics and derivative weaves. The weaver has to master it above all other weaves.

In plain weave the weft thread passes alternately over and under the warp threads (figure 1-24). The visual appearance of the weave, however, may be altered by the materials used. Whether the yarn is smooth, textured, thick, or thin influences the weave, as does the interaction between the warp and the weft. If the warp threads are close to each other, the weft does not cover them as completely as it does in other techniques such as pile weaves, tapestry, and warp-encircling techniques. Plain weave is the basis for lace weaves, laid-in weaves, and color patterns in which the warp and the weft show equally.

After you have warped the loom, weave a piece of flat cardboard or a smooth, flat stick at least 1 1/2" wide and longer than the width of the loom, referred to as a *tension stick*, into the warp above the bottom stretchers, using plain weave (figure 1-25). For a sample or a small experiment the cardboard might be woven over 2 threads and under 2 threads. This produces a sett of 4 pairs, which can be handled as though they were single threads. The pairs can be used as a sett of 4 threads to the inch and then separated for double-layer effects. This arrangement allows for spontaneity and adaptability to different ideas. A sett of 4 is very coarse: it is covered quickly and mistakes are more visible than in finer warps. The cardboard serves many purposes: the first rows of weft that are beaten against it are prevented from going down to the nails; it provides enough warp to knot and finish the ends when the piece is removed from the loom and stops the warp threads from pulling on the inside when the tension is released; it takes up any slack in the warp and

1-24. Plain weave is the basic weaving structure. One weft thread passes alternately over and under a series of single warp threads.

1-25. The tension sticks and the heading are woven into the warp in plain weave before beginning the design. (Photo: Robert Fields)

20

helps maintain a tighter tension. As the weaving progresses, the weft takes up the slack and the warp becomes tighter, so the cardboard can be removed to loosen the tension again.

Start by weaving a few rows of plain weave. These rows are called the *heading*, and they prevent the pattern from raveling when the piece is removed from the loom. A heavy, soft yarn is a good choice, and it can be removed when the project is finished or rolled under in a hem. The next rows may be any yarn that goes with the design and serve as a border.

A variation on plain weave that can be substituted in some situations that call for plain weave is *double basket weave* (figure 1-26). In this construction 2 weft threads pass alternately over and under 2 warp threads. Another variation is to weave a single weft thread alternately over and under 2 warp threads (figure 1-27). This is called *single basket weave*. The order and number of weft and warp threads may be changed in the same row to produce a textured effect (figure 1-28). When there are several rows of weft in the same shed, weave the weft either as a double thread or as a simple weft yarn that is repeated over and over in the same shed. To prevent the weft yarn from pulling out when it enters the same shed, encircle the warp selvage thread at the edge and continue weaving.

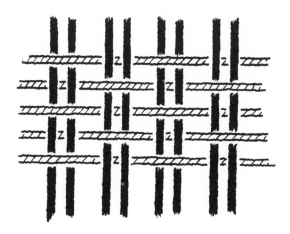

1-27. Single basket weave. One weft thread passes over and under consecutive pairs of warp threads.

1-28. Tina Kyrthe. Variations on plain weave and basket weave. The weave may be changed in the middle of a row of weft to produce a textured surface. (Courtesy of the artist)

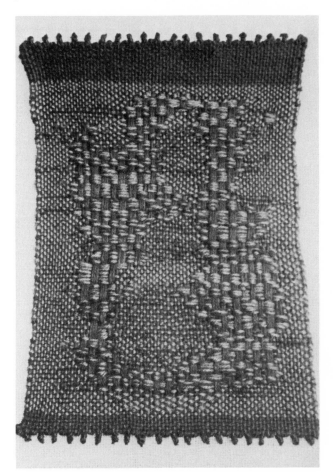

1-26. Double basket weave. Two weft threads pass over and under alternate pairs of warp threads.

The warp threads on the nail frame loom are manipulated by the fingers or by a threaded tapestry needle with a large enough eye to pass the yarn through. Most people prefer working with their fingers. The materials are pliable and easy to form. The weaving itself is simple: with your fingers or the threaded needle lift the warp to create the shed (figure 1-29), pass the weft through, and beat it into place. A comb with evenly spaced teeth, a fork, a tapestry comb, or your fingers works quite well as a beater. Both sheds can be manipulated with your fingers, or you can make one shed by weaving a shed stick into the warp, using plain weave (figure 1-30). A *shed stick*, or *sword*, is a smooth, flat piece of wood about 1 1/2" wide and the width of the loom in length, sometimes shaped like a broad sword. When the stick is turned at a right angle to the warp, it raises every other warp thread (figure 1-31). Pass the weft through, lower the stick, and beat the weft down (figure 1-32).

The nail frame loom does not really have a top or bottom. The direction is relative to the weaving, and the work may progress from both ends of the warp. The tension stick and the heading can be put in at both the top and the bottom of the loom. They help to keep the selvages of the piece even. You can weave from either direction, even with the loom turned over or reversed.

Never pull the weft threads straight across the warp. This will pull the edges in and produce an irregular edge. The edges tend to pull in slightly on both sides, but it is important to keep them straight. Pinch the weft at the selvages, hold it in place, and gently slant, arch, or arc the weft and press it down firmly. Work across the warp by arcing small portions of the weft and then beating them down. It is better to leave small loops at the sides than to pull the threads in too tightly. When the weft crosses over the warp in one direction, it is called a *pick*, *shot*, or *throw* of weft. Do not leave the ends of the weft threads hanging out on the selvages. Leave about 1 1/2" on the weft and weave it back at least three warp threads or 1/2" into the fabric. Trim the weft off after you have secured it with a few more rows of weaving. Other ways of ending a thread are discussed with the specific techniques.

If the selvages are a constant battle, place a wire the diameter of the warp thread along each edge from the top to the bottom stretcher and weave around it. The wire serves as a gauge and a reminder not to pull the thread in. Remove the wires when the piece is finished. Another aid in watching the edges and preventing them from pulling in is to tie a loop around each selvage and tie the ends of the loop togehter to the side of the frame. The loops slide ahead of the weaving as the work progresses and pull the end warp threads out just slightly as a reminder.

The very nature of weaving on a frame loom makes it time-consuming, but speed in production is not a criterion for the precision and craftsmanship of the piece or the quality of the design.

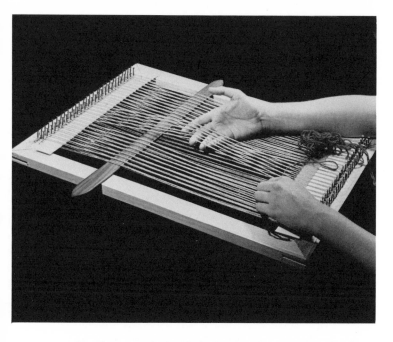

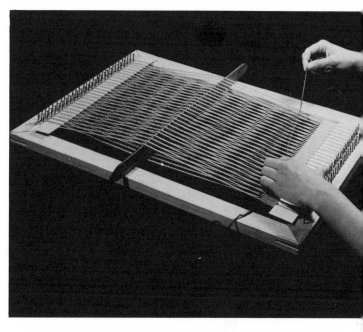

1-29. Finger-manipulated shed: select the warp threads with your fingers and lift them to produce a space, or shed, through which the weft yarn passes. The weft can be in a ball form or wound in a butterfly. (Photo: Robert Fields)

1-30. A shed stick, or sword, may be used for the second shed. It is inserted in plain weave. (Photo: Hector Garcia)

1-31. When the sword is turned on edge at a right angle to the warp, it creates a shed. Always slant the weft as shown. Weaving small sections at a time and arcing the weft help prevent the edges from pulling in too drastically. (Photo: Hector Garcia)

1-32. The sword presses the weft into place. Your fingers, a fork, or a comb with evenly spaced teeth may also be used to press the weft down. (Photo: Hector Garcia)

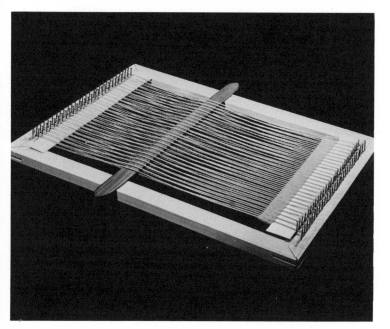

THE HEDDLE FRAME LOOM

The *heddle frame loom* employs a different method to create the two separate sheds necessary for plain weave, and you don't have to handle each warp thread with your fingers. The first shed is formed by turning the shed stick on its side at a right angle to the warp, and the second shed is raised by a series of warp-lifting devices called *heddles*, or *leashes* (figure 1-33).

In comparison to the nail frame loom, the heddle frame loom takes more time to make and has more parts—the heddle bar, the two warp-end bars, the shed stick, and the tension stick. However, it has the advantage of a weaving length twice the length of the frame (figure 1-34), and the sheds are easier to manipulate for laid-in weaves, lace weaves, and color patterns. Double weaves are not possible on this particular frame, since the weaving progresses from the bottom upwards on one side only.

Construction

In addition to the canvas stretchers needed for the frame, this loom requires four L-shaped brackets; sixteen wood screws, 5/8" × 6"; two machine screws, 6/32" × 2"; two machine screws 6/32" × 3/4"; two corner brackets; and three dowel rods, 1/2" in diameter and the length and width of the entire frame. Two dowel rods are used as warp-end bars, and the third as a heddle bar. The diameter and length of the screws and the dowel rods will vary, depending on the size of the frame loom. The dimensions given are suitable for a loom ranging from 16" to 24" in length. The larger the dowels, the longer the machine screws should be to compensate for the extra thicknesses of wood. There is a large assortment of sizes available at hardware and art-supply stores.

1-33. A heddle frame loom. (Photo: Hector Garcia)

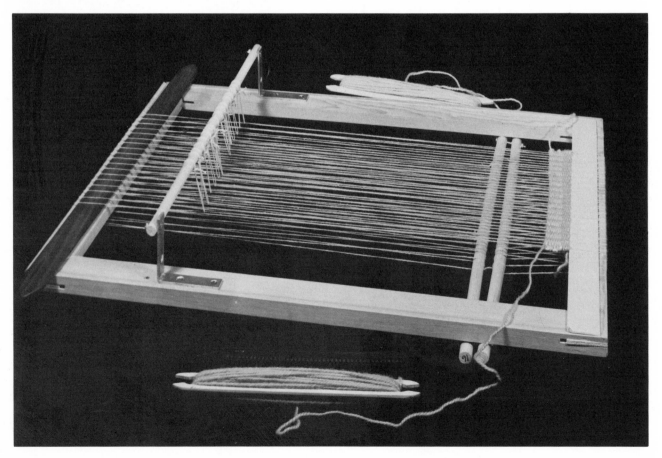

Put the frame together with the four canvas stretchers in the same way as for the nail frame loom. The corners must be reinforced by screwing down the metal braces. This prevents the frame from shifting and the warp from being pulled out of line, which would be a disaster while weaving.

After you have assembled the frame, file shallow notches 1/2″ apart on the top and bottom stretchers. Put them on the narrow top side of the stretchers (figure 1-35). The notches should be in a direct line with each other across the entire weaving width. They help to space the warp and to keep it in place.

The heddles on this loom are loops made from linen or cotton cord and hung from the heddle bar. The heddle bar is constructed from two 2″ metal corner brackets screwed to each side stretcher and one wooden dowel rod as long as the width of the loom, bolted to the top of the brackets with the 6/32″ × 3/4″ machine screws and nuts.

Place the corner brackets at the edge of each side stretcher and mark where the holes are to be placed. The bottom holes should be down about a third of the distance from the top stretcher. Drill two small holes on each side. It is important to screw the brackets on parallel to each other. Hold the dowel rod horizontally so that each end is over the holes at the top of the brackets. Mark the rod at these points and drill holes large enough for the bolts to pass through. The heddle bar is not screwed on until after you have wound the warp, at which time the heddles, the two warp-end bars, the tension sticks, and the shed stick are also added.

The two warp-end sticks should be as long as the frame is wide. Mark them 1″ in from each side and use a vise, clamps, or tape to hold the dowel rods together while you drill a hole large enough for the bolts straight through both rods. Put a machine screw 8/32″ in diameter and 2″ long through both rods at each end and attach a nut a the tip of the screw. The screw is a tension device: the warp can be tightened or released by tightening or releasing the bolt.

The shed stick is a flat, smooth piece of wood about 1 1/2″ wide and longer than the width of the loom. It should be strong enough to endure stress. Use two thin, flat pieces of wood or heavy cardboard the width of the warp to maintain tension.

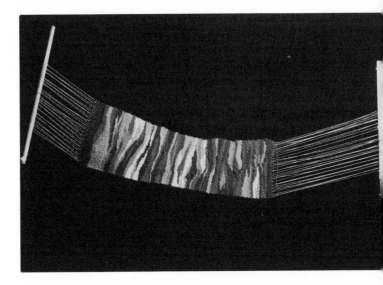

1-34. On a heddle frame loom the warp is twice the length of the frame, which allows a longer weaving length and longer warp ends for easier finishing. (Photo: Hector Garcia)

1-35. Put shallow notches on the narrow top side of the stretchers. (Photo: Hector Garcia)

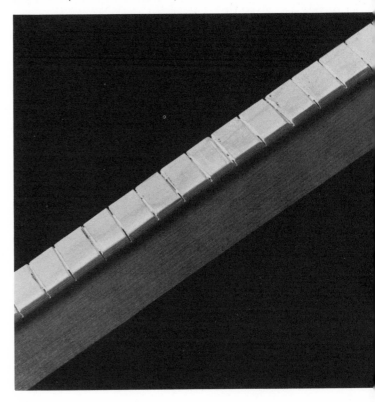

Warping

The warp on the heddle frame loom is double the length of the loom and continuous, and it can be revolved around the frame as the weaving progresses. The warping is done directly on the loom.

Tape the two warp-end bars, which are bolted or screwed to each other at both ends, to the back of the frame to keep them from shifting. The warp must be spaced as it is wound on. Distribute the threads according to the desired number of warp threads per inch. For a sett of 12 threads per inch, put 1 warp thread in a notch and 5 outside. A sett of 10 threads to the inch calls for 1 thread in a notch, 4 outside, and a repeat. A tapestry might call for 4 threads to the inch, or 1 thread in a notch and 1 outside the notch. Whatever the repeat, the sett should be continuous across the weaving width.

Center the warp in the frame if you are not using the entire width of the loom. Take the desired width of the final piece—say, 10"—and divide it in half. The result here is 5". Measure 5" from the center of the bottom warp-end bar to obtain the starting point.

When you are winding the warp, the yarn should be in a small ball or some other easily handled form that can be manipulated around the frame and passed between the warp-end bars. Tie the warp thread around the bottom warp-end bar with a clove-hitch knot (figure 1-22) at a point directly in line with the beginning sett mark. Warping is as follows (figure 1-36):

1. bring the warp thread down to the bottom stretcher and around it to the front of the frame;

2. up to the top stretcher and over it;

3. down the back of the frame to the top warp-end bar;

4. over the top of the warp-end bar and back up to the top of the frame;

5. down the front of the frame to the bottom stretcher;

6. over the bottom stretcher and back up to the bottom warp-end bar.

Continue the warp around the frame in this progression until you have wound the required number of threads. Tug on each warp thread as you pass it over the stretchers and tighten the tension by tightening the machine screws on the warp-end bars.

Some frame looms of this type use only one warp-end bar instead of two. The path is the same, passing over the end twice (see figure 1-37). The warp follows the same path as just described, passing over the same bar first in one direction and then in the other. As with the nail frame the warp should be tight, bounce back, and feel even all the way across. Adjust the threads if necessary by repeating the warping procedure, pulling down on the tight side, up towards the slack side, then down again. If the warp thread runs out, tie the end with a knot on the warp-end bar and start another thread beside it so that the thread continues in the same order.

To estimate the amount of warp needed, multiply the number of threads per inch by the total weaving width and by the length of the warp, as with the nail frame loom. In this case the warp is double the length of the frame. Remember that extra yarn is taken up when the warp passes over the stretchers.

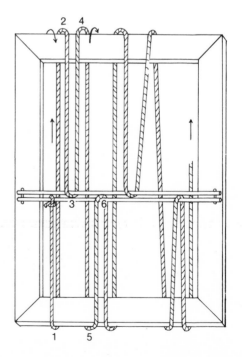

1-36. Warping the heddle frame loom. Whether one or two warp-end bars are used, the path of the warp thread is the same. If a new thread is started, tie the end onto the bar and start at the next point in the sequence.

Forming the Sheds

After you have completed the warping, attach the heddle bar to the top of the two corner brackets with the short machine screws and nuts.

The first shed is made by inserting the shed stick above the heddle bar (figure 1-38). Starting under the selvage threads, pick up thread 1 and all the odd-numbered threads. Check the warp by turning the shed stick on its side at a right angle to the warp. Every other warp thread should be raised.

The second shed is made with a series of heddles constructed of strong linen, carpet warp, cotton cord, or twine. Cut as many 10″ pieces of cord as there are even-numbered warp threads, or half the number of warp threads. Push the shed stick down against the corner brackets. It helps to distinguish the warp threads on top of the shed stick from those underneath it.

Slip the cut cords under the even-numbered threads in front of the heddle bar—the threads that are underneath the shed stick. Hold both ends of the heddle cords even and up towards the heddle bar without pulling the warp thread out of place. Pass each end of the heddle cord over the heddle bar, encircle the bar, divide the two ends in opposite directions, and bring them around from the back to the front. Tie the two ends together in a reef knot (figure 1-39). Each heddle should be tied on individually. Keep them all the same length. When the heddles are pulled up, the second shed is formed. The same cords can be cut off or untied and used again.

Insert tension sticks at both the top and the bottom stretchers, using plain weave. The first picks of weft threads are beaten down against the bottom tension stick. Weaving on the heddle frame loom moves from the bottom stretcher towards the heddle bar. Remove the tension stick from the bottom stretcher if you rotate the warp around the frame.

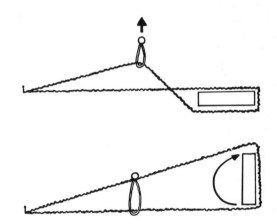

1-38. The sheds on a heddle frame loom.

1-37. A continuous warp wound around the frame loom and tied to one warp-end bar. (Photo: Hector Garcia)

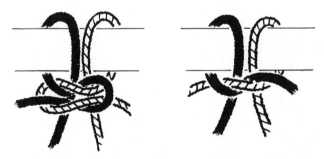

1-39. A reef knot is one way to attach string heddles to the loom. The string passes under the warp thread, forming a loop. The ends of the string pass from the front of the heddle bar to the back and then under the heddle bar to the front where they are tied together. The heddles may also be tied with any other secure knot.

27

If the weaving comes very close to the heddle bar and decreases the width of the shed, release the warp-end bars slightly and push them up towards the top stretcher. Remove the bottom tension stick and revolve the finished weaving around the bottom stretcher (figure 1-40). Stop revolving the warp when the last row of weaving is about 2″ from the top of the bottom stretcher (figure 1-41).

When you have finished weaving the piece, cut the warp off at both warp-end bars.

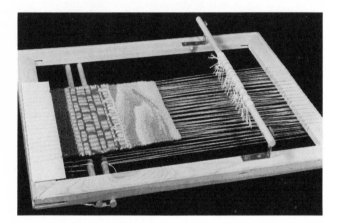

1-40. If the weaving comes too close to the heddle bar, remove the tension sticks and turn the loom over. Push up on the warp-end bars to revolve the weaving around the loom. (Photo: Hector Garcia)

1-41. Stop revolving the warp when the woven fabric is about 2″ from the bottom stretcher. The warp threads may need some adjustment: make sure that they are in proper sequence. It is not advisable to move the warp more than a few times, so weave as much as possible before moving the warp. (Photo: Hector Garcia)

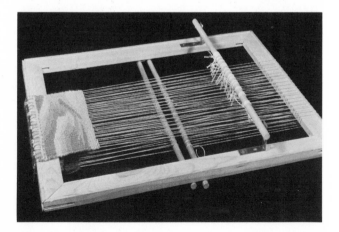

Weaving

To weave on a heddle frame loom, follow this procedure:

1. Open the first shed with the shed stick, moving the stick from the stretcher to the heddle bar (figure 1-42), then turn it on edge at a right angle to the warp (figure 1-43). Weave by passing the weft through the shed.

2. Close the first shed by pushing the stick back to the stretcher and beat the weft down (figure 1-44).

3. Open the second shed by pulling up on the string heddles and pass the weft through the shed (figure 1-45).

4. Close the second shed and beat down the weft.

The heddle frame has a narrow shed opening, but it is wide enough to use a flat shuttle for large areas of plain weave. Flat shuttles vary in length and are easy to handle. Do not use a bulky shuttle, because the weft will become too thick to pass through the shed.

Many variations are possible on the frame loom, since the equipment is simple and adaptable. Most people, once they understand the mechanics of the frame loom, construct a model to suit their own particular needs and preferences. The heddle frame loom can be used without the heddle bar or the shed device if you want only the double warp length. The warp can be wound continuously around the frame onto one or two warp-end bars. Some frame looms have grooved slots instead of nails. Others combine the nails with a heddle bar or bars. The more you read, see, weave, and study, the more ideas and suggestions will occur to you on how to build a simple loom.

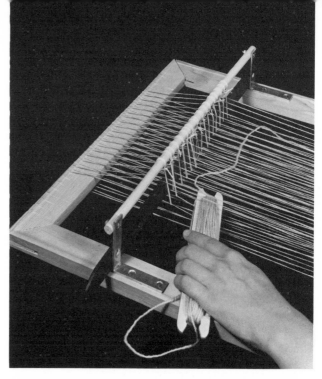

1-42. To open the first shed, slide the sword from the top of the loom down to the heddle-bar brackets. Return the sword to the top stretcher before opening the opposite shed. (Photo: Hector Garcia)

1-43. Open the first shed by turning the sword on edge at a right angle to the warp and insert the weft. A flat shuttle is ideal for this type of loom, since the weft generally moves in a continuous straight line from selvage to selvage. (Photo: Hector Garcia)

1-44. Close the shed and press the weft down with a comb, a fork, or your fingers. (Photo: Hector Garcia)

1-45. Open the second shed by pulling up on the string heddles. They are pulled up in groups. Pass the weft through the shed, close, and beat down into place. (Photo: Hector Garcia)

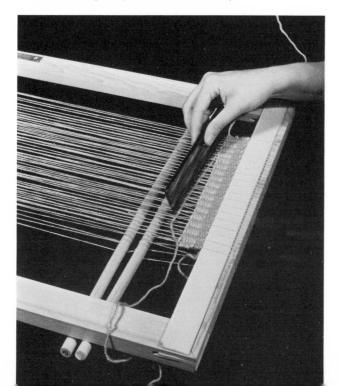

Weaving covers a vast area with countless ramifications and applications. There are many philosophies. The frame loom is meant to be a simple tool, a vehicle, a way to open your mind and free your imagination without being hampered by complicated procedures. The fewer mechanical devices there are to deal with, the more freedom there is in design and in manipulating weaves by hand. The frame loom is not a substitute for other looms—and the techniques in this book are not intended to replace other weaves. The frame loom and its possibilities are intended to be an accompaniment that enriches.

I consider the frame loom to be a weaver's sketchbook of samples, tests, explorations, and experiments. A painter prepares for a complete and final work with drawings and studies that help him or her to understand the nature of the subject and to discover the forms that best convey an idea. The weaver should also make a series of studies with fibers to help him or her understand the nature of the materials and media and to investigate the many ways of giving visual expression to an idea (figures 1-46 and 1-47).

1-46. *Earth* (study). Jane Redman. Tapestry weave, handspun thick-and-thin yarn, 6″ × 9″. (Photo: Hector Garcia)

1-47. *Earth*. Jane Redman. Tapestry, 27″ × 36″. The idea for this landscape was developed from the smaller study. The scale changes substantially: what could be expressed with a few knots or rows of tapestry in the study now requires larger areas and more definite shapes. (Photo: Hector Garcia)

CHAPTER 2.

YARNS AND COLORS

One of the first important and pleasant experiences in weaving is to select your yarns—the raw materials from which the weaver creates as well as the source of many inspirations. Yarns lend personality, life, energy, and vitality to your work. The final piece depends a great deal on the yarns chosen at the very outset. The accessibility of fibers from all over the world and the many combinations of color, size, texture, and weight offer a variety of choices that is very exciting and almost overwhelming.

The best way to begin is to collect as many different kinds of yarn as possible, if only in small amounts at first. Yarn is left over from every project, and it can be saved and added to a gradually growing inventory. Even very short pieces can be used in some manner: a 3″ length, for example, may come in handy for a precut pile or a fringe. It takes time to accumulate a large collection, but the object is to have a wide range of yarns available for experiments and samples.

Choosing yarns is a decision that blends the sense of touch with the sense of seeing. By using his hands and eyes the beginner soon becomes aware that in addition to texture and color yarns possess other properties—strength, elasticity, sheen, resistance to abrasive wear and sunlight. Each type of yarn has a different origin and an inherent uniqueness that is a study in itself.

FIBERS AND YARNS

Yarns are made by twisting and spinning natural and/or man-made fibers together to form a continuous strand that has a specific thickness, strength, and other desired qualities. *Natural* fibers include plant fibers, animal fibers, metal fibers, and mineral fibers. *Synthetic* fibers do not occur naturally: they are chemical compounds made by man in the laboratory. They are produced from such materials as coal, petroleum, wood pulp, salts, and cellulose, a substance found in the cell walls of plants.

All fibrous materials pass through different stages of cleaning and preparation before the fibers are extracted and loosely rolled into soft balls of *roving*, from which the yarns are spun. Yarns are composed of either filament or staple fibers. *Filament* fibers are primarily man-made. They are extruded from a machine in one unbroken length, measured in yards, sometimes in miles. Silk is the only natural fiber that is classified as a filament fiber. When a silk cocoon is unraveled, it may measure thousands of yards. Yarns formed from filament fibers are either *monofilament*—one single strand—or *multifilament*—two or more filaments twisted together.

Staple fibers include all the natural fibers except silk, although short ends of silk from broken

2-1. *The Annunciation.* Commissioned by Francesco Gonzaga, attributed to artists of the Court of Mantua. Tapestry weave; wool, silk, linen, and gold threads; Italian, 1506–1519; 72″ × 46″. (Courtesy of the Art Institute of Chicago)

cocoons may be spun together to create a staple yarn. Staple fibers are short—they are measured in inches or fractions of inches—and must be spun to form a yarn. Synthetic fibers are sometimes cut into shorter lengths and spun.

Both filament and staple fibers are twisted during spinning to hold the fibers together in a yarn. The amount of twist required varies according to the fiber. Roving has little or no twist; crepe has a very high, tight twist. The first twist creates a *singles* yarn—yarn spun in only one direction. The direction is either clockwise, called an *S-twist*, or counterclockwise, called a *Z-twist*. When two or more singles are combined, they form a *ply*—a two-ply yarn is a combination of two singles; a three-ply yarn, of three singles, and so on. S-twist and Z-twist singles are combined in a ply yarn to keep the strands interlocked. A *cable*, or *cord*, yarn is produced by twisting two or more plied yarns together.

Fine, hard, twisted yarns are considered *threads*. Textures are created not only by the fibers themselves but also by the tightness of the spinning, the angle and direction used to form the singles, and the interlocking of the plies.

Handweavers tend to prefer yarns made from the natural fibers—linen, cotton, wool, and silk. They possess a warmth and a liveliness that is enjoyable to work with. Asbestos, fiberglass, and metallic fibers obtained from gold, silver, aluminum, and copper are also considered to be natural. During the Renaissance it was a common practice to add gold or silver threads to a woven tapestry (figure 2-1), and some contemporary weavers still add metallic threads to their tapestries (figure 2-2).

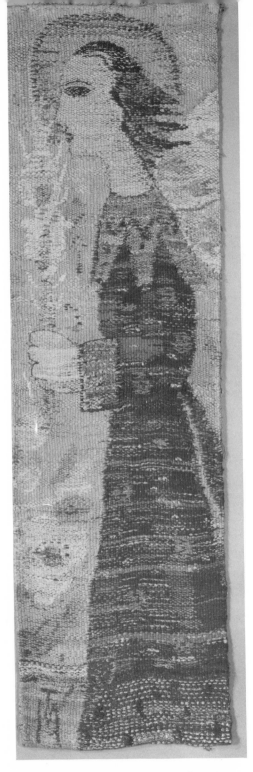

2-2. *The Angel with the Red.* Martta Taipale. Tapestry weave, wool and metal threads, Finnish, 1961, 60 1/2″ × 17 1/2″. (Courtesy of the Art Institute of Chicago)

Synthetic yarns are usually bright, intense, and shiny, but they can also resemble the natural fibers. Rayon, the first synthetic, was developed as a substitute for silk. Synthetics are widely used in industry and in commercial fabrics in the form of very fine threads but are also available in coarser sizes and textures. They are not as elastic as natural yarns.

Synthetic and natural yarns can be woven together into *blends*, and they often complement each other. Both natural and synthetic yarns can be made into *novelty*, or *specialty*, yarns, which are plied into loops, curls, nubs, and slubs. Many novelty yarns have three elements: a core, a decorative yarn, and a binder twisted in to hold the yarns together. Novelty yarns are characterized by spaced irregularities in color, texture, size, and twist. They usually have a very textural effect.

Yardage

To estimate the yardage in a pound of yarn, it is necessary to become familiar with the varying yarn counts of different fibers. When fibers are spun together, they are given a number that is determined by the amount of yarn it takes to make up a pound. This number, referred to as the *yarn count*, indicates the size and thickness of the yarn. Different standards are applied to each fiber: there is no universal system.

Filament yarns are measured in deniers. A *denier* is equivalent to the weight in grams of 9,000 meters of yarn. The higher the number, the coarser the yarn: a 20-denier yarn is twice as coarse as a 10-denier yarn.

The denier system is based on weight per length and is applied to silk and synthetic fibers. Yarn spun of staple fibers is measured by the number of *hanks* required to make a pound of yarn: the higher the number, the finer the yarn.

The cotton count, for example, is based on a formula determined by the number of yards that can be spun from a pound of raw cotton. A pound of cotton can be spun into 840 yards of single-ply #1 yarn, and a hank of cotton equals 840 yards. Single-ply #2 yarn is half the size, producing two hanks, or 1,680 yards per pound, and so on.

The counts of other staple-fiber yarns are calculated in a similar manner. If there is no indication as to how many yards are in a pound of packaged yarn, it is possible to determine the yardage from a standard of a specific length per pound for each fiber. The spun-silk count is the same as the cotton count—single-ply #1 yarn yields 840 yards per pound. Single-ply #1 run wool (cut and unplied) yields 1,600 yards per pound, while worsted wool (plied) yields 560 yards per pound. The linen count is based on a formula of 300 yards, called *lea*, per pound of raw flax. The jute, hemp, and ramie counts are calculated on the linen count.

When 2 or more single-ply threads are twisted together to make a plied yarn, the ply is indicated by a number. A 20/2 cotton thread, for example, is composed of 2 threads of #20 single-ply yarn twisted together. To obtain the yardage, multiply the count by the yarn number and divide by the ply: 20/2 cotton thread yields 8,400 yards per pound; 10/3 cotton thread, 2,800 yards per pound.

Two different systems are applied to silk, one for spun silk and the other for reeled silk—filaments wound off the cocoon. For spun silk the yardage is figured on the basis of the number of 840-yard hanks needed to make a pound of yarn. The number of plies does not affect the count: the yardage in a specific number yarn stays the same whether the yarn is plied or not.

If 450 meters, or about 492.2 yards, of a reeled silk weigh 1 denier, or .05 grams, the silk is a #1 yarn. There are 4,464,528 yards in a pound of #1 silk. To find the number of yards in a pound, divide the denier number into 4,464,528.

The yardage of novelty yarns is difficult to determine. If it is not indicated on the package, it should be requested from the supplier. Although a weaver who works on a small frame loom is usually not too concerned with the amount of yardage of a yarn, this information is helpful in comparing prices and important in planning large projects.

Warp Yarns

Not all yarns are suitable for the warp. The warp is pulled, stretched, and under tension. The yarn must have enough tensile strength to endure a great deal of strain and wear. Any material—cotton, silk, wool, synthetics, or blends—may be used if it has been spun for strength. The staple length—the length of the fibers—determines the strength of the yarn: the longer the fiber, the stronger the yarn. A hard,

tightly twisted yarn is a better choice for the warp than a soft, loosely twisted yarn or an unplied singles yarn, which will fray with handling. To avoid frustrations, there are a few guidelines that you should follow.

A smooth, strong, nonabrasive yarn that does not cling works best as a warp in tapestry and rug weaves, since it allows the weft threads to be packed and beaten in tightly. Thickness or heaviness is not an indication of the strength of a yarn. A very fine synthetic can appear fragile and yet be very strong. The opposite is true of some thick yarns that seem strong but in fact are weak. If a quick pull or snap breaks a thread, it is not suitable. A warp yarn should not break or fray easily. The best yarns for a frame-loom warp that is to be covered are cotton, carpet warp, and linen. Linen is a good choice even though it has a slight tendency to buckle and stretch. Wool can be used if it is not pulled and stretched until the yarn has lost all elasticity. Plied spun-silk yarns work well but are expensive, so they are not a wise choice for a warp that is going to be covered. There is a wide range of synthetics and blends that are suitable. A wool-and-nylon blend makes an excellent warp.

Thick, textured yarns can be used on a frame loom for a warp that is not going to be covered (figure 2-3). One of the advantages of the frame loom is that novelty yarns and nubby, fuzzy, irregular, or hairy yarns are not limited only to the weft.

2-3. Bib Neiman. Pillows, woven on a frame loom with a warp of heavy thick-and-thin handspun yarns. (Photo: Thomas England)

2-4. *Fish.* Virginia Virak. Double-layer weave: the warp threads were left unwoven and float on top of the bottom layer, which is woven in tapestry weave in a pattern of different colors and textures. (Photo: Hector Garcia)

2-5. Beads or other objects may be strung on the warp while it is being wound on the loom. The beads easily slide along the thread and can be distributed across the weaving width according to the design. (Photo: Hector Garcia)

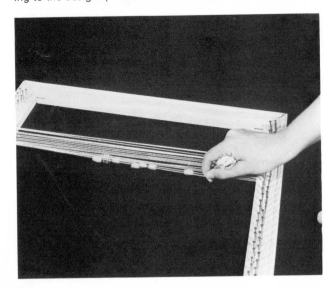

The metal beater and heddles on a harness loom are abrasive and would cause these yarns to fray. The eye of the metal heddle is too small for some of the thicker threads to pass through. If string heddles are used on a frame, they can be made larger to accommodate the thicker, textured threads. Any novelty thread can be used unless it is too thick and cumbersome to manipulate.

2-6. Jane Redman. Sampler. The beads in the warp slide up and down until they are secured in place by weaving. A slit-tapestry technique works best, since it provides a woven base for the objects and holds them in place when the weft crosses over into another color area. The slits can be on either side of the object. The thread on which the object is strung is included in the weaving after the height of the slit is established. (Photo: Hector Garcia)

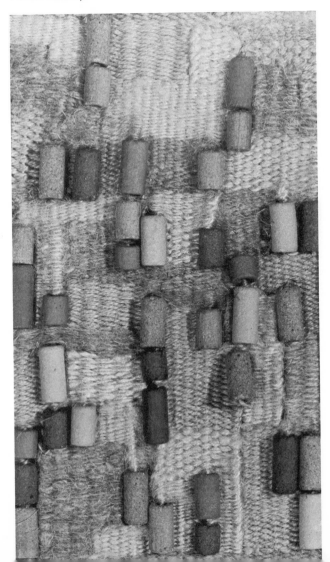

If the warp is intended to show, it must be considered as part of the visual design as well as the woven structure. The combination of colors and textures in both warp and weft will affect each other and must be treated accordingly (figure 2-4). If only the weft is creating the design, as with tapestry and knotting techniques, the warp is completely covered and the color is not important. White is usually used, but a natural color such as beige or gray is restful to work with and causes less eye strain.

When you are warping a frame loom, objects such as beads or cylinders can be slipped onto the warp threads and distributed across the weaving width (figure 2-5). They will slide up and down until they are fastened in place by the weaving and incorporated into the design (figure 2-6). Small objects may also be strung on the weft threads and incorporated into the weaving (figure 2-7).

2-7. Beads, shells, or other objects may also be strung on the weft. String the weft yarn with the objects, then pop them in between the warp threads onto the surface. Placement is a matter of choice, and the objects will slide along the weft until they are secured in the weaving. (Photo: Hector Garcia)

Weft Yarns

Design, technique, and function determine the choice of weft yarns. They are not under the same tension as the warp yarns, so there are fewer restrictions. Each yarn possesses different characteristics, so you will have to choose weft yarns individually for a specific treatment in a project. Some materials are long, thin, and flexible, so they are easily woven, beaten, twisted, and knotted into the warp. Others are less elastic, even rigid. The selection is vast—it includes all the sizes, weights, colors, and textures of yarn, thread, string, rope, ribbon, cord, leather, paper, fabric, wire, metal, plastic, and wood, as well as any branch, vine, leaf, stalk, stem, fur, or feather from nature. Your imagination will come up with many ideas, but do remember to take into account the construction of the weave, the durability of the yarn, and the suitability of the yarn to the object (see figures 2-8 through 2-11). Nothing should appear as an afterthought. The color and texture of the yarn should be harmonious with the function and concept of the piece. It should be a montage of different materials put together effectively rather than appearing as though beads or feathers were stuck on after it was finished as an afterthought.

Avoid using large quantities of yarns intended for other purposes, such as knitting and crocheting. They tend to be too soft and do not pack down properly, producing a woven piece that does not have the right firmness. By manipulating the yarns between your fingers and arranging them in twists and loops, you will discover how they feel and handle.

Once you have selected your materials, group the yarns and lay them out side by side to see which colors and textures complement each other. Sometimes your first selection may seem satisfactory, but it is worthwhile to take the time to explore other combinations and relationships in a relaxed atmosphere. When you approach design in this manner, your experiments will often suggest a whole series of new ideas and associations. The knowledge and experience you gain are worth the few extra minutes. Try to select yarns that reinforce or enhance your personal vision.

2-8. Jane Redman. Small sample with chaining. The wooden pieces are held in place by wrapped warps, and the background is also woven. (Photo: Hector Garcia)

2-9. Josette Lebbin. Study with wrapped warp threads and ceramic pieces. (Photo: Robert Fields)

2-10. Jane Redman. Hanging, incorporating feathers and beads. (Author's photo)

2-11. Tapestry weave, with branches, rocks, and money plants incorporated into the design. (Courtesy of Gwynne Lott)

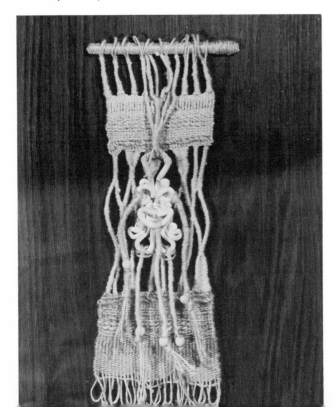

Yarns and Weaves

The quality and character of the materials that you use and the manner in which you handle them determine the character, quality, appearance, and function of the final piece. How a project looks and how well it suits its use depend on the interaction of the yarn with the weave. Some constructions, knots, or other ways of manipulating a yarn bring out its character better than others.

A soft, spun weft yarn is pliable and will cover the warp quickly if it is used in a heading. Sturdy, hard, spun yarns add firmess and body, especially in a plain weave. Some yarns are not as visually effective if they are packed tightly and should rather be woven loosely, fringed, or knotted to allow enough space to be seen. The function of the piece—whether it is intended to be cuddled, as toys and pillows are, hung, draped, worn, or mounted on the wall—is an important consideration in choosing your materials. Stiff, scratchy textures do not feel pleasant to the touch or comfortable close to the body, yet they might be very effective as visual texture in a wall hanging.

The effective weaver understands the nature of the materials, respects the disciplines of the craft, and has mastered a range of techniques to work with. Each new project presents a different set of problems and therefore requires a different set of solutions. The importance—and the fun—of experimenting and exploring to see how yarns respond and interact cannot be stressed enough. This is the creative learning situation. Warp the nail frame loom with several warps of different-weight yarns and different setts. Change the wefts to create totally different effects. Try to weave a sample that gradually moves from a smooth to a very rough texture. Observe how close or how far apart the weave is. Try to control the spacing by changing the weft (figure 2-12).

2-12. The frame loom may be warped in a sett of 4, 8, 12, or 16 threads per inch to accommodate a variety of wefts and techniques. Any suitable flexible material may be used as a weft. (Photo: Hector Garcia)

COLORS

Selecting yarns means selecting colors. No discussion of yarn would be complete without mentioning this important element. Of all the factors involved in weaving color is easily one of the most elusive and baffling to work with. Color seems to shift, change, express, imply, and deceive. It is never seen in isolation as it really is; instead it is perceived and understood only in relation to surrounding colors and textures. Size, shape, and lighting influence color. Color can be an intimate personal expression, yet it is open to change with every trend in fashion and taste. We are bombarded with colors, yet we use only a few words to describe them.

There are many interesting theories of color, but the best way to deal with it is to become aware of what happens when colors interact with each other. Color is a visual experience; it depends on perception. The choice of colors depends largely on subjective feeling and observation, not just on theory or verbal description. Color can be described in scientific terms, but it still remains difficult to handle, since it is emotionally and psychologically evocative. Colors carry meanings and create sensations that we respond to.

The French impressionist-pointillist painters Paul Signac and Georges Seurat applied the principle of optical blending of colors, which had been developed by Chevreul of the Gobelins tapestry workshop. The weaver also mixes colors optically—from visual combinations of different-colored yarns—rather than from pigments, as a painter usually does. If strands of two or more colors are woven together, they seem to blend at a distance.

Visual Properties

To control color, it is necessary to understand its special visual qualities. All colors can be described in terms of hue, value, and intensity. *Hue* refers to the name of a color as it appears in the light spectrum and in rainbows. White light may be broken down into the separate hues of the spectrum—red, orange, yellow, green, blue, indigo, violet—with a prism. Black and white are not real colors—black is the absence of color; white, the presence of all colors—but are considered as such in everyday terminology. A hue is the pure state of a color, unaltered by other colors.

On the traditional color wheel the position and family of a color is denoted by its hue. The color wheel represents the abstract idea of pure colors. It is a system used to show the relationships between colors. The color wheel, or color spectrum, only helps in understanding color harmonies. Each person will think of a different blue if he or she is asked to visualize a pure blue or a blue with which they are familiar. The colors used from wheel to wheel will also vary, but the system remains the same.

Red, yellow, and blue are considered *primary colors* on the color wheel, because they cannot be obtained from other colors. When red and yellow pigments are mixed in equal proportions, the result is orange; yellow and blue create green; blue and red create purple. Orange, green, and purple are *secondary colors*. There is also a set of *tertiary colors*, a group of six variations obtained by mixing a primary color with the adjacent secondary color.

Starting at the top of a twelve-color wheel and continuing clockwise, the colors are yellow, yellow-green, green, green-blue, blue, blue-purple, purple, purple-red, red, red-orange, orange, and orange-yellow. The twelve hues are of equal value and intensity. The next larger color wheel would be twice as large, each color being mixed equally with the one next to it. Colors that are next to each other on the wheel are called *analogous*, or *neighboring*, *colors*. Colors directly opposite each other are called *complementary colors*.

Value refers to the lightness or darkness of a color in relation to black and white. A red, for example, can range from a very light pink to a very deep, dark red, but all these variations are included within the same family, or hue. The dark tones of a hue are called *shades*, and the lighter tones are called *tints*. The normal value of a hue is that in which it appears in the prismatic spectrum. Blue and violet are usually darker in value than orange or yellow, but every color has a vast range of value changes, and some values of yellow are darker than very light values of blue.

Something very exciting happens in a woven piece when the yarns and weaves create shadows and value changes. The actual physical structure of the yarn interacts with the structure of the weave to create patterns of light and dark within the same color. Texture also affects color: the same color in a soft, fuzzy wool or mohair looks very different in a rayon or linen. A shiny surface reflects light and lightens a color, while a soft pile surface absorbs light and darkens a color. Two close values of the same color used together will enrich the surface of a piece.

Intensity, *chroma*, or *saturation* refers to the brightness or dullness of a color. The purity of a color is determined by its freedom from gray. The greater the purity, the closer the color is to the original hue. Colors that are mixed with a dissimilar color tend to be duller—less saturated with the pure color. The difference is obvious when different colors thought to be from the same family are compared to each other. A yellow mixed with a violet appears much duller than a pure yellow. Value and intensity are interrelated, since a color is simultaneously dark or light and dull or bright. In addition to hue, value, and intensity colors tend to appear *warm* or *cool*. Reds, oranges, yellows, and even most browns are considered warm. Blues, greens, and purples are considered cool. Some colors, such as yellow-green and red-violet, seem to reflect both warm and cool qualities, since they are combinations of warm and cool colors.

Warm colors tend to advance and appear larger, while cool colors seem to recede and appear smaller. When they are put side by side, they create a back-and-forth movement as the eye moves from one color to the other. Opposing colors that share no common hue also have this effect. Black and white, for example, demand equal attention from the viewer. So do complementary colors—orange and blue, green and red, yellow and purple. When opposing colors are placed next to each other, the constrast may become so intense that the edges of the colors seem to vibrate. Complementary colors mixed together in small areas produce a gray. If the complementaries clash or are too strong, reduce the intensity by choosing a duller color from the same family.

Related colors that share a common hue blend and melt together. They are softer around the edges and less demanding to look at. They tend to modify each other. Opposing colors always intensify each other and make the contrast seem even greater. Putting a bright and a dull color side by side will make the dull color seem duller than it really is, and the bright color brighter. Using dark and light colors together makes the dark color appear darker, and the light lighter. The degree of change depends on the degree of contact: the more a color comes into contact with its opposite, the greater the change. The maximum change is obtained when one color is completely surrounded by another.

To work out color combinations, twist the yarns together or wrap them around a card to see how they look together. Two yarns of different hues will give the optical impression of a third color: red and yellow together, for example, will create an orange cast. See if the colors seem compatible. Which colors dominate? Do they advance or recede? Do they enhance each other, or is one distracting? Are they harsh or soft? Really look at the colors. Carry them around and study them under different lights, especially in natural sunlight.

Relationships

There are a few simple experiments that are helpful in observing how colors interact with each other. Place a small paper square of a secondary color alternately within larger squares of the component primaries. A green will appear yellower against blue and bluer against yellow. Observe whether the colors appear duller, brighter, warmer, cooler, larger, or smaller.

A similar study may be done with value. Place a small paper square of medium value alternately against a light-value background and a very dark background. Observe what happens (figure 2-13). Try this experiment with strands of different colors and a variety of different yarns as backgrounds. The background yarns can be in any form—skeins, spools, balls, etc. Notice how the color changes with each background.

The following color combinations are offered as guidelines for harmonious relationships. You must use your own judgment, however, in deciding which colors are compatible and work best in a piece. The color harmonies express an abstract relationship between pure colors on the color wheel. The interaction of colors in a specific instance depends on which particular red, green, blue, yellow, orange, or purple is being used.

The simplest use of color is a *monochromatic* scheme. Only one color, with its value changes, is used. Sometimes white, gray, and black are added.

The natural earth tones are also easy to work with. They should not be thought of as just grays and browns, as they come in a full range of subtle variations, and all grays show traces of some color, either warm or cool.

Analogous combinations use a sequence of two or more neighboring hues on the color wheel. All the warm or all the cool hues can be used successfully.

A *complementary* scheme is composed of hues that are opposite each other on the color wheel. In a *split-complementary* scheme, instead of using the direct opposite of a color, the hues on either side of the complementary color are used. This provides three colors to work with. A *double-complementary* scheme includes four colors—two pairs of complementary colors. The harmonies have more variety when they include value changes.

Color is forceful: it attracts attention and reinforces the whole feeling of a piece. The only way to gain mastery over color is to constantly work with it, to look at colors for warmth, coolness, value, and intensity. Study the colors—analyze the changes in the appearance of a color against different backgrounds. Concentrate on colors and try to deter-

2-13. Value changes. A small woven square with a medium value of gray is placed on both a dark and a light background. The light background makes the gray appear darker; the darker background makes the gray appear lighter. (Photo: Hector Garcia)

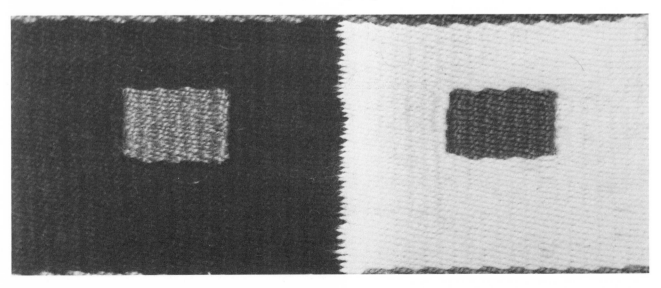

mine how much blue, red, or yellow is in each one. In small projects aim for unity: do not divide a piece into too many separate shapes and colors. Contrast light and dark and warm and cool shades of the same color.

An excellent experiment in weaving colors is to make a color blanket. A color blanket can range from the entire spectrum on the color wheel to only a section of the spectrum. It can be made from several values of a few colors or a monochromatic range of values from light to dark. For your first sampler start with about six colors that are of equal value and intensity.

Two factors are involved in weaving a color blanket: (1) the warp and weft must show equally, and (2) the weft must be woven across in the same order of colors and with the same number of threads as the warp. A plain-weave or basket-weave structure or a variation of one of these works well.

The sett of the warp should be at least 8 threads to the inch, and the warp should be heavy or close enough so that the weft does not cover it. After you have selected your colors, wind about 8 or 10 warp threads of each color on the frame loom. Tie on the first color in the warp sequence, wind it around the desired number of nails, tie it again, and cut it off. Start the next color on the adjacent nail and follow the same sequence. Warp the entire piece in color sections in this manner.

The key to the success of the project is in the interaction of the colors. As the weft travels across the warp, it interacts visually with every color in the warp. This enables you to see how a color looks in combination with other colors in the spectrum. It is a way of determining which colors look best together. The perception of color is a subjective experience that can be developed through practice and observation.

After you have woven several color blankets, it is fun to try designing plaids. A plaid is constructed in the same manner as a color blanket. The weft is woven in the same color order and with the same number of threads as the warp. The colors in the warp can be in many different widths and in any order. This project is an exercise in proportion as well as color (figure 2-14).

2-14. In a plaid both the warp and the weft show. The weft is woven in the same color sequence as the warp, which results in a combination of colors . Notice how the value of the weft appears to change in relation to the light and dark warps. (Photo: Hector Garcia)

CHAPTER 3.

PLAIN-WEAVE TAPESTRY

The tapestry technique has become almost synonymous with the large mural, architectural wall hangings that it is most often used to produce (figure 3-1), and the term "tapestry" is sometimes mistakenly applied to any fabric that is hung on the wall, regardless of the technique. The shapes in a tapestry design are formed by the interlocking of the warp and weft: they are not added—as embroidery, for example—to a surface that has already been woven.

Tapestry is traditionally a type of weaving in which the weft yarns completely cover the warp, unlike other weaving techniques in which both warp and weft show. In contemporary wall hangings areas of woven tapestry are sometimes intermingled with areas of exposed warp to produce solid woven and open nonwoven shapes (figure 3-2) or with knotting and pile techniques (figure 3-3). The interaction of color and texture in both warp and weft has to be taken into consideration in design combinations of this sort.

Tapestry is a variation of plain weave. It is based on the use of alternate warp threads and an off-balanced distribution of warp and weft. The warp is widely spaced, and there are more weft threads per inch. Since the weft is pressed down to cover the warp, the spaces between the warp threads must be wider than the width of the weft yarn. The sett of the warp is dependent on the thickness of the weft. Most tapestry warps on a frame loom are between 4 and 8 threads per inch.

The weft covers the warp on both the front and the back, producing what are referred to as *ribs*. Ribs are ridges inside the weft that follow the same path as the vertical warp threads. They look like slightly raised hills with a valley on either side. The texture of the ribs produces a highlight on top and a deeper shadow in the valley.

3-1. *Pomona.* Designed by Sir Edward Burne-Jones and William Morris. Tapestry weave, wool, English, late 19th century, 64″ × 36″. (Courtesy of the Art Institute of Chicago)

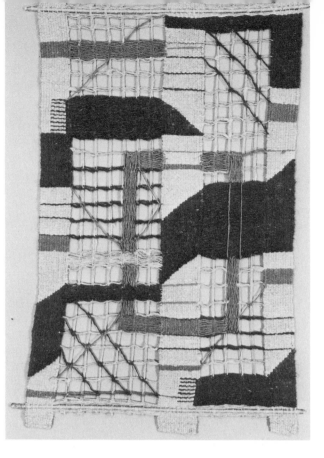

3-2. *Fisherman's Knot.* Cynthia Schira. Tapestry weave, wool, American, 1968, 30″ × 20″. (Courtesy of the Art Institute of Chicago)

3-3. Noreen Rubin. Mask in rya, plain weave, and double weave. (Photo: Hector Garcia)

The weft yarns seldom pass in one continuous line across the entire weaving width of the warp, unless they are being used at the top and the bottom for a border or a heading. In some designs, such as stripes, columns, and checkerboard patterns, or large background areas (figure 3-4), the weft may cross the entire piece. Usually, however, a tapestry is composed of many separate areas of contrasting colors and shapes, within which the weft is woven back and forth. The structure of the tapestry is determined by the manner in which the wefts meet at the edge of each shape and are joined together.

There are as many insertions of different weft yarns across a row of weaving as there are color and pattern changes in the row (figure 3-5). Individual bobbins or small finger-wound skeins called *butterflies* are used to insert each color and to keep the yarn in order (figure 3-6). Shapes in the design can be developed independently of each other rather than simultaneously in a horizontal line. The butterflies are simply left hanging until they are needed again or until a specific shape is finished.

3-5. Sampler in tapestry weave with interlocking techniques. The different wefts are kept in order with butterflies and bobbins. Because the wefts interlock, they develop as a continuous line. (Courtesy of Gwynne Lott)

3-4. Rebecca Wold. Tapestry weave. (Photo: Hector Garcia)

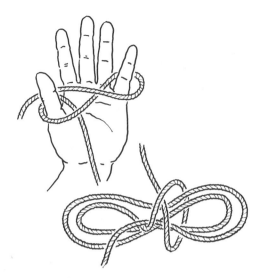

Remember that each shape has a separate weft. Do not skip around to different shapes with the same weft. A new shape can be introduced at any point on a row. Make sure, however, that you develop the design at the same rate so that no awkward spaces are left to weave in below an overhanging shape.

To end a weft yarn, leave it on the back of the tapestry and cut it short (figure 3-7) or pull it down inside the rib at the edge of a shape (figure 3-8). A tapestry needle with a large eye and a dull point is a necessary piece of equipment for finishing weft ends. Firm weaving will keep the ends from coming out.

3-6. A butterfly, or finger-wound skein, is used to keep the weft in order. Tie the skein as shown, leaving the tail hanging on the side of your thumb.

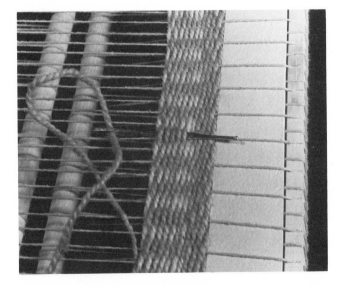

3-7. To finish a weft yarn in tapestry, either leave the end hanging on the back of the piece and clip it short, or pull it down inside the tapestry rib. (Photo: Hector Garcia)

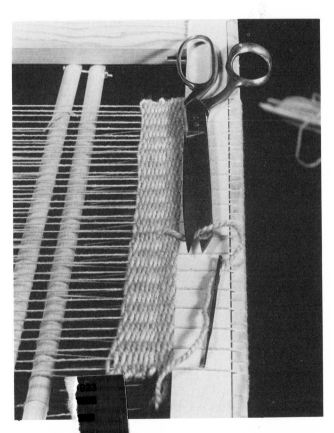

3-8. Pull the [ ] least 1″ inside the rib with a tapestry needle and c. [ ] (Photo: Hector Garcia)

The infinite variety of shapes possible and the freedom of placement and color make tapestry a hand technique. The complete submissiveness of the materials and the adaptability of the technique lend a great potential of individual interpretation to tapestry designs. The only important rule to remember is to maintain the plain-weave structure: otherwise the weft will not cover properly, and the warp will show as a mistake.

Even though the process is almost as ancient as thread interlacing and weaving itself, forming the shapes is so easy, direct, and basic that tapestry weaving is continually being used with new insight and new expression. Since tapestry can be used to produce so many different forms, it is referred to as a method of *pictorial* rather than *pattern* weaving, which deals with loom-controlled, repeated units of design (figure 3-9). Pictorial weaving differs from pattern weaving in concept and purpose. Loom-controlled units appear at regular intervals because the loom is programmed to select a specific combination of warp threads. In tapestry, however, any repetition of line, shape, color, or texture is selected by the weaver. Tapestry is the most uninhibited of weaving techniques. Once the technique is understood and mastered, the hand and mind can work together unimpeded.

Tapestry brings the weaver into an intimate relationship with his personal vision; it enables him to communicate his feelings and ideas visually.

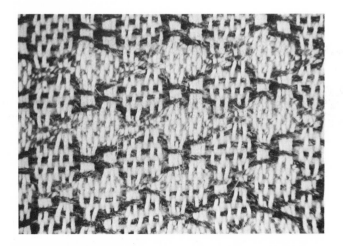

3-9. Loom-repeated pattern. The loom is threaded to select the specific warp threads needed to form the construction. (Author's photo)

3-10. *The Holy Family*. Artist unknown. Tapestry weave, wool, Flemish, early 16th century. (Courtesy of the Art Institute of Chicago)

Tapestry may be used to produce a piece that has the same presence as any other work of art in which the combination of content and design command attention and require perception and thought. The fact that weaving is used to produce commercial fabrics by the yard has at times blurred the recognition that fabrics can be totally individual and that the interlocking of threads can be used to create images (figure 3-10). The ability to create was once considered to be magic. Everyone who creates is still a magician who is able to transform simple materials into something elaborate and beautiful, to produce illusions, to give charm and mystery to the ordinary and life to the inanimate (figure 3-11).

3-11. Studio of Ramses Wisca Wassef. Tapestry, linen and wool, Egyptian, 1971. 62″ × 16 1/2″. (Courtesy of the Art Institute of Chicago)

THE TAPESTRY LOOM

The tapestry loom is simply a vertical frame equipped with side devices that hold a heddle bar. The large, upright tapestry looms are sturdy and durable. They may have cloth and warp beams, but usually most of the design is in view. Sometimes there are treadles to manipulate the sheds, but the fingers may also manipulate both the weft and the warp threads (figures 3-12 and 3-13). Since only two sheds are required, tapestry may be woven on any type of loom. A tapestry woven on a vertical upright loom is referred to as *haute lisse*, or high-warp, tapestry. A tapestry woven on a conventional horizontal handloom is referred to as *basse lisse*, or low-warp, tapestry.

THE FRAME LOOM

A nail frame loom is ideal for weaving, designing, and planning tapestries since it allows freedom of choice, is easy to warp, and permits a great deal of spontaneity within a few mechanical and structural limitations. The weaver is in direct control of the piece and has the pleasure of direct contact with the fibers, yarns, and materials.

Your first projects should be done as exercises to help you discover the potentials and problems involved in tapestry weaving. Bold, simple designs in a few colors work best (figure 3-14). You will gain confidence and understanding through work and practice.

If you have never done a tapestry, a small nail frame loom that is easy to handle is good to start with. A well-lit, quiet, pleasant working area is important for concentration. After a short time your fingers will move more quickly, shapes will become easier to plan and form, and the process will begin to feel natural and comfortable.

The best approach is to begin with samples in order to understand the structures involved and to learn how to form yarns into shapes. Before you start a major design, experiment with different combinations of shapes, colors, and textures to discover the range of possibilities available. More ways of organizing a design will come to mind as you gain experience with each new project.

3-12. *Attitude de l'ouvrier pour commencer l'ouvrage.* Gobelins. Haute-lisse tapestry, illustration from *Encyclopédie Universelle*, volume II, by Denis Diderot, 17th century. (Courtesy of the Art Institute of Chicago)

3-13. Jan Groth at the loom in his studio. Denmark. (Courtesy of Jan Groth)

For your experiments two or more warps can be wound onto the same loom side by side. Simply wind the first warp on the loom with the desired number of threads per inch and the desired width, then tie it and cut it off from the spool, ball, or skein. Skip a nail and start another warp. Several pieces can be done side by side as a means of comparison. Try the same design in different colors, textures, and sizes or work on as many different shapes and patterns as possible. The frame loom takes very little time to warp and is a quick way of testing ideas. Different warp threads and setts can be explored at the same time. Try the same design with different weights of thread to discover if the thickness or closeness of the warp has an effect on the weft shapes.

The Warp

A wool warp is not advisable for a first endeavor. Strong, smooth linen, carpet warp, or cotton should be used, and the warp should be spaced 4 threads to the inch. This is a wide sett that covers easily, produces bold shapes, and allows you to see exactly what is happening. A sett of 8 may be used later for finer details.

The Weft

If you are not doing traditional tapestry, any yarn can be used for a weft if it produces the desired effect, but it is best to start with two-ply tapestry wools of one consistent size. Wool is rich in both color and texture. It is enjoyable to touch and work with. The idea of the first few samplers is to get the feel of the yarns and the technique.

After you weave in the heading, you are ready to begin. If you have set up several different warps, treat each warp separately and give it a separate heading. The tension stick may go all the way across the loom.

3-14. Virginia Virak. Tapestry based on simple modular repeats of squares and rectangles. The single patterned square attracts the eye of the viewer. (Photo: Hector Garcia)

COLOR CHANGES

A wide variety of effects can be achieved by making simple color changes in plainwoven wefts. Alternating single lines of two different colors will produce a narrow vertical column. This occurs because every other weft passes over either the odd-numbered threads or the even-numbered threads. If two rows of the same color are woven consecutively, the pattern is altered at that point, and the position of the colors is reversed. A checkerboard pattern is created by alternating colors in every other row of weft and then reversing the position of the colors. The size of the columns or checks is determined by the size of the length and the width. The length can extend along the entire piece, or it can be altered by occasionally weaving two rows of the same color and changing the position of the colors. The width is determined by the sett of the threads. A sett of 4 will produce columns 1/4" wide, and a sett of 8 will produce columns 1/8" wide (figure 3-15). On the frame loom it is possible to manipulate a sett of 8 either as single threads or as double threads. There is a wide selection of grids, checks, vertical lines, and columns that can be used effectively (figure 3-16).

3-15. Pillow in tapestry weave. The change in the width of the checks depends on the change in the sett of the warp threads and whether they are single, double, or triple. (Courtesy of Sharon Shattan)

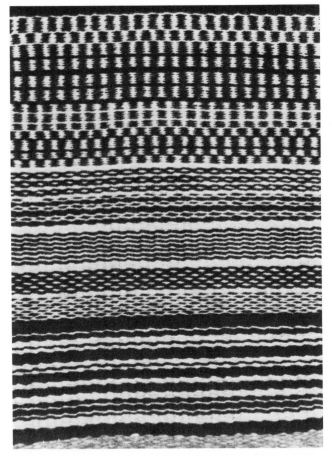

3-16. There are many effective combinations of grids, checks, columns, mottled effects, and illusionistic effects, such as shading, which are produced by alternating rows of color. Using two rows of the same colors, for example, creates a solid line. The rotation of weft colors changes the position of the weft yarn—whether it always passes over the same thread or sometimes passes under it. (Photo: Hector Garcia)

The selvages, as always, need careful handling. Since the first weft crosses the second weft at the edge of the piece before entering the next shed, the two wefts must wrap around each other at the selvage. This prevents you from skipping over the end warp threads when you are using alternate weft threads (figure 3-17).

Many more effects can be obtained by manipulating two or more colors in different proportions and sequences. Horizontal lines are produced by weaving at least two weft rows of one color and alternating them with another two rows of a different color. Since two picks of weft are used for each color, the stripes are of equal width. Wider horizontal stripes are formed by weaving several rows of the same color before changing to another color. A mottled effect is created by blending together different widths of thick and thin stripes, emphasizing the distribution of color and the light and dark values. The illusion of shading is obtained through the closeness or distance between the stripes. Solid shapes can be woven on a mottled background.

If you are using two, three, four, or more rows of the same color, carry the weft alongside the selvage and use it again. When you cut the weft off the butterfly, weave the end back into the fabric or pull it down inside one of the ribs with a needle. The weft is not usually carried alongside the selvage for more than 1/2". A helpful trick to avoid leaving two weft ends on the edge is to start the first end inside the tapestry and weave out to the selvage. The end inside the design can be left hanging in the back, and you have only one end to weave back in.

3-17. To weave columns, always pass the dark weft over the same warp thread; and the light weft, under the same warp thread. Since the rows alternate, the wefts must interlock as shown at the edge. To change the position of the colors, weave in two rows of either color in between alternate single rows of color.

FORMING SHAPES

There are three ways to form shapes in tapestry: (1) the slit method, (2) interlocking weft threads around each other, and (3) interlocking separate wefts around the same warp thread. The slit method is very versatile, and the interlocking methods produce a strong structure that is ideal for functional projects. A different weft is wound in a butterfly, on a bobbin, or in a small ball for every color change in a row. Each weft is used until the shape is completed. The colors are inserted in plain weave. The tails of the wefts may be left hanging on the back of the tapestry, woven back into the fabric (if they are hanging on the edge by the selvage), or pulled down inside a rib with a tapestry needle. The needle should have a dull point and a large enough eye for heavier yarns to pass through.

The Slit Method

The slit method is not only a tapestry technique but one of the oldest Near Eastern rug weaves, used for kilim carpets. A slit is a space between two color areas that do not interlock and are not joined together. It may be straight or on the diagonal in a stair-step pattern. Straight slits are used to form vertical shapes—squares and rectangles (figure 3-18); diagonal slits, to form triangular shapes (figure 3-19).

To make a straight slit, weave the weft across the warp until it reaches the last warp thread at the edge of that particular shape. Bring the weft out to the surface of the warp, turn it around, and pass it through the alternate shed back to the original starting point. The warp thread at the edge of the shape is encircled automatically (figure 3-20), and

3-18. Tamma Farra. Tapestry weave with slits. (Photo: Robert Fields)

3-19. Hanging, tapestry weave. The triangular shapes are formed with diagonal slits. (Courtesy of Gwynne Lott)

a long, narrow slit is left at the points at which the weft returns to the same place. Do not pull the weft tight, or the edges of the shape will pucker. Allow enough slack in the weft so you can beat it down.

The weft is easier to control in small amounts and in small areas. Weave in a small amount and then beat it down into place. Always arc the weft. Changes in the position of a shape and the introduction of other shapes will shift the meeting points of a particular weft back and forth so that it is very rare for a slit to travel all the way up a tapestry. The structure of the fabric is strengthened by shifting the joining points and using different warp threads as change points for design areas.

A straight slit leaves a clean-cut line, but if you don't want open spaces in your piece, sew the slits together when the tapestry is finished. The slits are often left open on a small tapestry, however, as part of the design and structure (figure 3-21).

Diagonal slits are produced gradually on the right and/or left sides as the wefts move over consecutive warp threads in a regular progression. The first weft moves over 1 warp thread, while the adjacent weft moves back 1 warp thread (figure 3-22). The shapes appear to be interlocked, but there are small openings that are hardly noticeable.

3-21. Susan Schneider. Hanging in tapestry weave with straight slits. (Courtesy of Gwynne Lott)

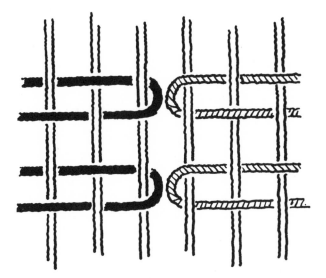

3-20. Straight slit.

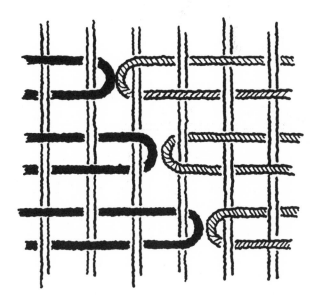

3-22. Diagonal slit.

55

The slant of the diagonal is controlled by the number of rows of weft used before the weft moves to another warp thread. There can be many rows of weft. The more rows there are before moving over to the next warp thread, the coarser the incline will become until it turns into a series of steps.

Diagonal slits can be used to make many different triangular shapes of various sizes. An equilateral triangle is achieved by first weaving in the base and then moving inward at an equal rate on both the right and left sides. The weft might move over 1 warp thread with each row or in a series of steps. The inverse is true if you start from the point of an equilateral triangle: the weft moves outward 1 warp thread at a time on each side.

Many other geometric and irregular shapes can be created by combining squares, rectangles, and triangles. Triangles can even be manipulated to form circular and oval shapes. Lozenges and rounded shapes are built up and molded by pushing the weft threads higher or lower with your fingers. You can weave two triangles base to base to make a diamond shape, for example, and then push it down to form a curved or lozenge shape (figures 3-23 and 3-24). Very often this form of tapestry weaving uses a technique called *eccentric weft*. The weft yarn changes from its usual horizontal position and moves at an acute angle to the warp as it passes over curved and rounded shapes.

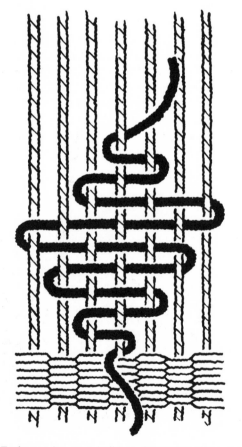

3-23. To form a lozenge, build up the center of the shape gradually with extra picks of weft. Manipulate the form by molding the edges with your fingers or weave a loose diamond and push it down.

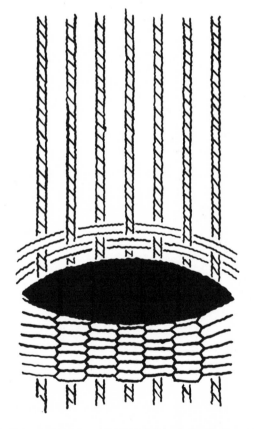

3-24. Once a curve has been established, the weft must travel over it rather than in a straight line. If the curve is accentuated, the weft becomes eccentric: it travels at an acute angle to the warp rather than in a horizontal position.

Circular shapes are often very effective even though they seem unsuited to the vertical-horizontal axis of the weaving structure (figure 3-25). Build them up through a series of small steps and inclines and push them around until they appear rounded (figure 3-26). It is hard to control curves on a coarse warp, since the weft thread has to move over 1 warp thread at a time. With a sett of 4 threads, for example, the weft moves over 1/4″ with each progressive pick. A perfect circle is impossible. Some textured yarns will disguise the steps used to form the circle.

The major advantage of the slit method is that shapes may be developed that are structurally independent of each other. Instead of developing a design row by row, you develop it shape by shape. You are free to form one shape or group of shapes before another. This is especially important if you are experimenting without a predetermined plan.

The only point to remember is to always maintain the plain-weave sequence when a new weft enters a color area or a new change point is established. New rows of weft must always enter the opposite shed from their predecessors, or the warp will not be covered and will show as a flaw. Sometimes it is necessary to weave an extra pick across a shape or to remove a pick in order to maintain the right sequence. There is usually no problem with equal-weight wefts. Working with different-weight wefts is harder at first, since a shape will require either more or fewer picks of weft in order to eventually re-establish the horizontal line in adjacent shapes. The weft does not move from one shape to another until the first shape is finished.

If a shape overhangs an unwoven area, use a tapestry needle to weave in the bottom. Try to avoid this situation if possible, since the spacing can become rather awkward.

3-25. Patricia Warner. Hanging in tapestry weave. (Courtesy of the artist)

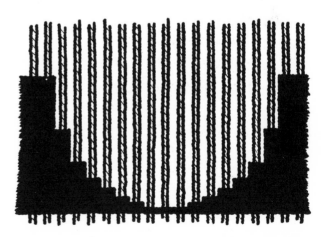

3-26. A circular shape is formed from a series of steps. The coarser the warp, the more difficult it is to control the curve. If the shape around the circle is woven first, the circle is easier to control, since the weft can press against the surrounding threads.

Interlocking Weft Threads

Weft yarns can interlock with each other in the spaces between the warp threads either vertically (figure 3-27) or diagonally (figure 3-28). Wefts moving through the shed from opposite directions loop around each other at the meeting space and then return in the alternate shed to their own side and color area. They should loop in the same direction and order each time to keep the joining smooth and to prevent irregular spots of color from appearing. This method works best if only a few rows of weaving and a few simple shapes are involved. Shapes cannot be built independently of each other, however, since a given weft must interlock with the weft from the adjoining shape. The shapes then develop horizontally line by line.

Interlocking Over Warp Threads

In this method different wefts are carried around a common warp thread but do not loop around each other. Again, the connection can be either vertical (figure 3-29) or diagonal (figure 3-30). One weft comes to the change point, turns around the warp thread, and returns in the alternate shed. Then the opposite weft comes across the warp to the same warp thread, wraps around it, and returns to its own color area. The edges along the joinings are feathery and sawtoothed in appearance. This method is sometimes referred to as *brick interlocking*, as it can resemble bricklaying.

Another form of interlocking around common warp threads is called *dovetailing*. The interlockings are formed by regular (figure 3-31) or irregular (figure 3-32) groupings of weft threads. The same warp thread may be used consistently as a change point, or the change point may shift back and forth from one warp thread to another.

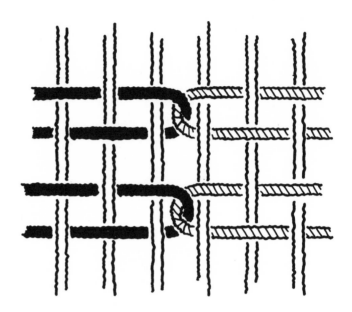

3-27. Straight interlocking of common weft threads.

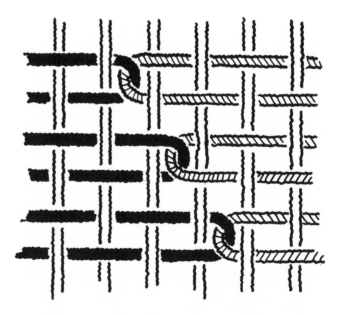

3-28. Diagonal interlocking of common weft threads.

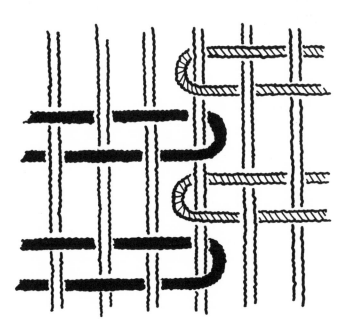

3-29. Straight interlocking over a common warp thread.

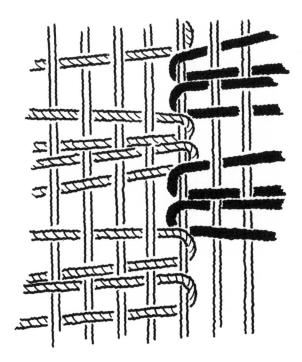

3-31. Dovetailing in regular groups.

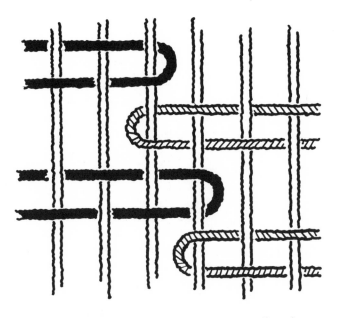

3-30. Diagonal interlocking over a common warp thread.

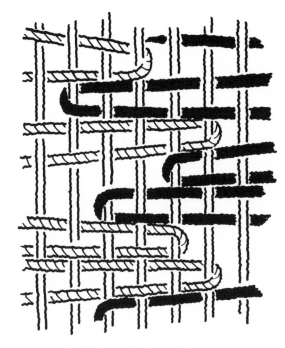

3-32. Dovetailing in irregular staggered groups.

FORMING LINES
Hatching

Hatching is a means of creating feathery horizontal lines in a solid-color area (figure 3-33) and of blending colors (figure 3-34). A weft travels partway across the warp into an adjoining color area, turns around, and returns in the alternate shed back into its own color area. Hatching is used with thick and thin lines and shifting change points (figure 3-35). The opposite wefts keep crossing into the neighboring color areas (figure 3-36). It is important to start the two wefts for the two color areas in the same shed. Starting either from the edges or the center, begin by weaving one weft across into the opposite color area; turn the warp thread around at the change point and return in the opposite shed to the original color area. Then weave the opposite color. The two wefts are always woven from opposite directions. There will sometimes be a slight buildup in the center. If such a distortion occurs, weave in a few extra picks of weft at the sides before entering the opposite color area.

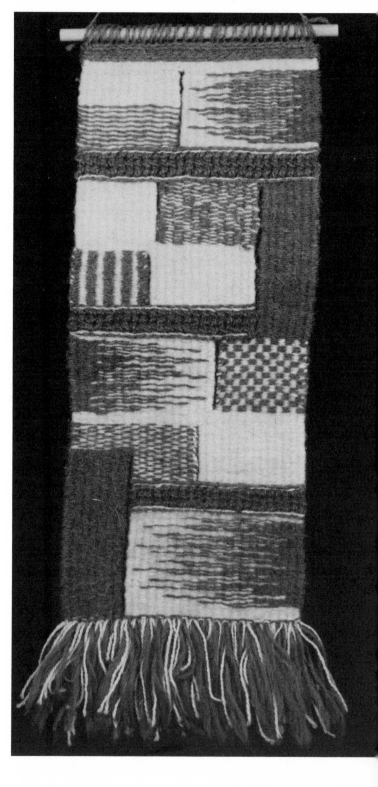

3-33. Nancy Sullivan. Hanging in tapestry weave, with hatching, slits, plain-weave color changes, and Greek soumak as accents. (Photo: Hector Garcia)

3-34. *The Resurrection* (a reduced version of the eighth in a set of ten tapestries from the *Redemption Series*). Artist unknown. Tapestry weave, wool and silk, Flemish, c. 1500–1510, 243″ × 176 1/2″. In this traditional tapestry technique the piece was woven sideways and hung at a 90° angle from its original position on the loom. The hatching used to shade the forms was easier to weave as a fine horizontal line but was hung vertically, producing a fine vertical line. (Courtesy of the Art Institute of Chicago)

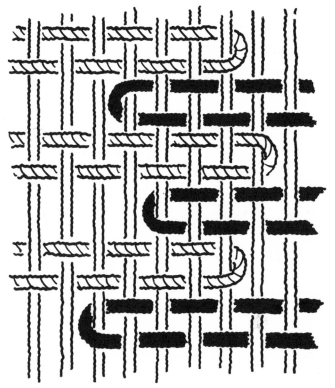

3-35. Hatching.

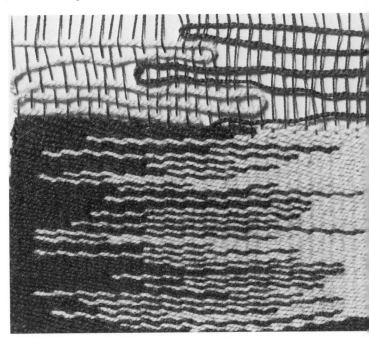

3-36. Hatching. (Photo: Hector Garcia)

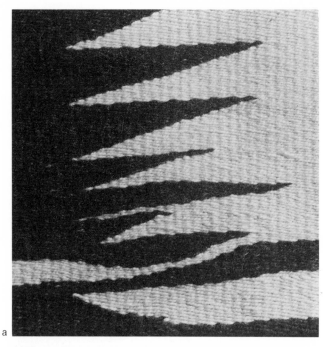

a

b

3-37. Hachures, horizontal (a) and vertical (b). The vertical design could be woven horizontally and hung sideways. The vertical direction gives height to the design and pulls the viewer's eye up and down the piece. (Photo: Hector Garcia)

Hachures

Hachures are flamelike shapes instead of lines, but they serve the same function: to break up solid-color areas (figure 3-37). Hachures may be regular or irregular. They might be compared to interlocking fingers. They are effective both in strong, contrasting colors and values and in soft, subtle blendings of colors.

Outlining

To outline a triangular shape, weave a diagonal line in plain weave along the edge and contour of the shape with a contrasting or heavier yarn. Contrasting wefts are particularly effective in outlining ovals and lozenge shapes (figure 3-38) and in emphasizing the contour. The weft simply follows the edge of the shape and is woven in on a diagonal.

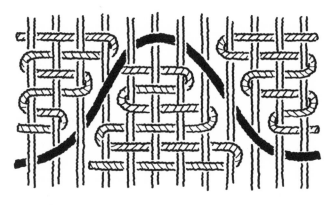

3-38. Outlining with plain weave.

CONTOURING

The contour of a woven piece does not have to be a square or a rectangle. Just as shapes and figures can be produced within a tapestry, the same principles can be applied to the shape of the finished project itself.

Although the warp is rectangular in form, the warp threads at the edge of the piece can be left unwoven. By moving the weft yarns at the edges inward in a regular progression on both side, for example, a triangle is produced. Many other geometric shapes can be formed simply by leaving the outer warp threads that define that shape unwoven (figure 3-39). When the piece is finished, cut the threads in the desired shape. The unwoven warp threads can be knotted, woven back in with a needle, or pulled down inside a rib with a tapestry needle (figure 3-40). Never pull a warp thread back into its own rib, however, or the weft will unravel.

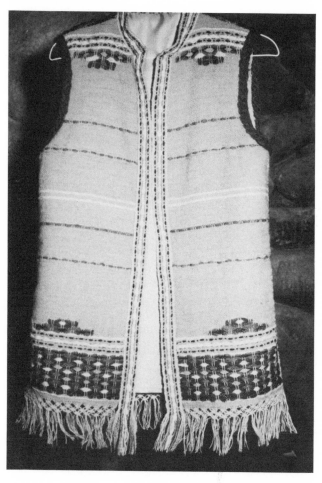

3-40. Suzanne Gaston-Voute. Finished jacket, with Danish medallions used as an accent. (Courtesy of the artist)

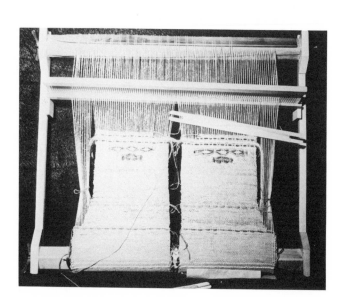

3-39. This coat is shaped on the loom by moving the weft in and leaving the warp threads that define the contour unwoven. (Courtesy of Suzanne Gaston-Voute)

THE TAPESTRY CARTOON

After you have woven several samplers to explore the possibilities of shapes, colors, and textures and to develop control over the tapestry technique, it is interesting to try the very controlled, traditional approach of weaving a design from a tapestry cartoon. A *cartoon* is a full-scale model of the design. All the shapes, patterns, and forms are drawn on paper, and the textures and colors are indicated. The cartoon is not a picture or a painting: it must be prepared with a sensitivity to the weaving process and the inherent characteristics of fabric. It is important to realize that the cartoon will be translated into yarn and to plan it with a consideration of the possibilities available. The design in the cartoon always looks different when it is woven. The yarns have a physical texture, form, and depth, and the colors a richness that add life to the flat two-dimensional cartoon.

Designing the Cartoon

There are several points to consider when you design a cartoon. One of the most important is that the fineness of the warp determines how much detailing is possible. The shapes must be clearly outlined, and the flat areas of color indicated.

The outlines of the shapes are easier to follow if they are composed in the weft direction. The minimum width of vertical lines in plain weave is 2 warp threads, and stripes, hatching, and hachures can only be worked horizontally (figure 3-41).

The direction of the weave must be taken into account, since it will greatly influence the design: it is a major factor in determining the choice and placement of lines, shapes, stripes, hatchings, and hachures. Shapes and lines running horizontally across the cartoon are easier to weave than vertical ones, since it is easier to weave a narrower line with the weft moving across the warp. Stripes and hatchings have to be placed horizontally in the cartoon, but you may plan on turning the finished weaving at a 90° angle from the original position on the loom. The weft will then run vertically, and the warp horizontally (figure 3-42).

If the design lines are intended to be vertical, weave them horizontally and hang the piece vertically. The weft threads are closer together, form the stronger part of the tapestry, and do not

slip. The cartoon should be fastened under the tapestry sideways while the weaving is in progress (figure 3-43). The composition of the cartoon determines the direction in which the piece should be woven. Other factors are the desired direction of any slits and ribs and which side of the design will be shown.

The ribs have a marvelous ability to catch light and create shadows. The designer-weaver must decide how to best use this phenomenon. If slits are hung vertically, they have a tendency to loosen from the surroundings. The sagging can be controlled and used as part of the work, or the slits can be hung sideways or shortened.

3-41. Ricki Epstein. A minimum of 2 warp threads can be used to weave a vertical line. Among a series of slits the narrow bands create an effective texture. (Courtesy of Gwynne Lott)

3-42. *Village.* Judy Cohen. Plain-weave tapestry, done from a cartoon and hung sideways at a 90° angle. (Photo: Robert Fields)

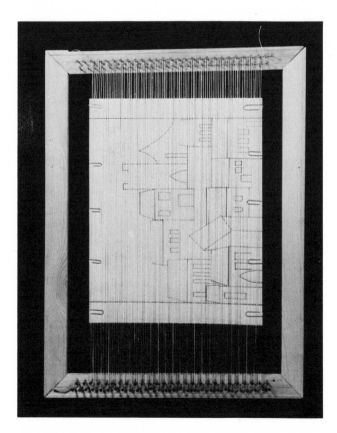

Tapestry was traditionally woven backwards. The reverse side faced the weaver, since the weft ends, butterflies, shuttles, and bobbins hung loose on the back. So many combinations of techniques and individual approaches are being used today that tapestries are usually worked with the design side facing up and hung with the warp threads running vertically. On a small frame loom, however, tapestry can be worked in any direction. The loom can be flipped over or reversed if there is a change in design or technique.

Transferring the Design

Once you have determined the direction of the cartoon in relation to the weaving, tape or paperclip it behind the warp. On a small frame loom you can place the cartoon under the warp and ink it in on the warp. Use waterproof ink to indicate the colors and changes in shape so that it will not run it if becomes damp. Hold the pen point against the warp and outline the design. Try to cover most of the warp thread so that you can see the ink even if the thread twists around. The whole warp can be drawn on, since it will be covered. Make sure that the design is facing in the same direction as the finished work.

The frame loom is ideal for tapestry cartoons, as all parts of the design can be seen at the same time. On a harness loom the woven warp is wound underneath onto the cloth beam, so it has to be unrolled to be seen. Even with a cartoon color and texture change a design, and it is important to see how the parts relate to each other.

Some weavers do not work from a cartoon or even from a sketch or a drawing. It is possible to work directly on the loom without a predetermined design when you have developed an awareness and a sensitivity to the visual elements and their relationship to the colors, shapes, textures, and patterns as they evolve on the loom.

3-43. The tapestry cartoon is a simple rendering of the shapes in the design. Changes in color or texture can also be indicated. The cartoon can either be drawn on a piece of paper that extends from stretcher to stretcher and is tacked down to the sides of the frame, or it may be clipped to the warp. Allow for the heading and the finishing before starting the design. (Photo: Hector Garcia)

CHAPTER 4.

OTHER CONSTRUCTION METHODS

Alterations in the appearance of a woven surface can be produced simply by using a wide selection of textured yarns in a plain weave. The texture and the height of the surface plane may also be changed by using different woven constructions. An awareness of the range of techniques available is necessary in order to control the physical structure of the piece, to achieve the desired visual effects, and to solve problems that might occur. The methods explained in this chapter offer the weaver a wide range of varying heights, textures, and surfaces. They can be used by themselves or in combination with other weaves to supply contrasting areas or accents (figure 4-1). Each method has a specific characteristic that makes it important. Some of these techniques were originally used for rugs but have now found a multitude of new uses and applications.

4-1. *Spider*. Sue Feulner. A combination of textures is produced by combining a rya pile weave with wrapping. (Photo: Robert Fields)

4-2. Various textures of low pile, with cut and uncut loops. (Photo: Hector Garcia)

4-3. Long, shaggy precut pile, knotted in the rya technique. Precut strands may be altered to any length. (Photo: Hector Garcia)

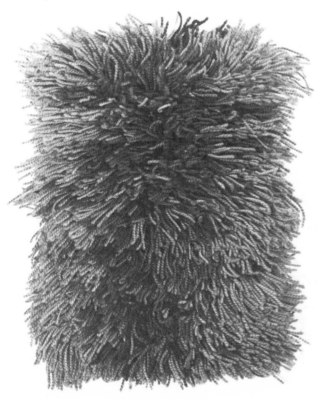

PILE WEAVES

An excellent example of how a simple principle can be expanded to obtain many different results is the pile weaves. They form a raised surface that adds a third dimension to a flat weave. The added height pulls the image out from the lower plane towards the viewer. You can create a low pile, in which the surface is only slightly raised (figure 4-2); a high pile, which is usually a long shag (figure 4-3); or a loop, which projects from the surface (figure 4-4).

4-4. Uncut Ghiordes loops on a plain-weave background. Pile surfaces are effective in creating simple designs, basic geometric structures, and contrasting textures. (Courtesy of Gwynne Lott)

Pile weaves are formed by adding extra warp or weft threads above the surface of the fabric during weaving. They may be cut or looped. On a frame loom pile weaves are usually formed by the predominant weft threads and are called *weft-face piles*. They are made from either a continuous yarn (uncut pile) or from lengths of yarn (precut) that are knotted individually on the warp. Ranging from a short, tightly controlled surface to a high, shaggy surface, the pile may be soft and luxurious—similar to velvet and fur—or a coarse, thick fringe. Any flexible material can be used. The pile may be short and shaped in low relief close to the surface or long—the length can vary from a fraction of an inch to several feet. If the pile is long, the threads can be easily braided, knotted, or otherwise manipulated into any number of forms. Piles may be looped, hand-knotted, or ready-made, such as a chenille weft that is woven into the warp instead of being knotted or pulled up. The chenille weft is tufted and appears to be a short, close pile. The pile effect of chenille is achieved through the construction of the yarn (figure 4-5).

4-5. Jane Redman. Double-layer construction. The plainwoven chenille weft appears to be a short pile weave due to the tufts in the yarn. (Photo: Hector Garcia)

Looped Piles

A looped weft-face pile is easily achieved by pulling loops up from the weft. The loops may vary in size, and they can be used to form spots of texture, shapes, rows, or groups (figure 4-6). The basis of the technique is plain weave, and several rows of plain weave, called the *ground*, are needed as a foundation. A heavy yarn should be used for the loop weft, and another yarn—either the same or lighter—for the plainwoven structure and as a binder in the background. The weft that is used to form the loops is woven in rather loosely. The loops progress from the side of the warp opposite the butterfly, bobbin, or shuttle that the weft is wound on.

The weft that passes over the warp threads is pulled up onto a gauge by your fingers or a crochet hook (figure 4-7). You can use different-sized gauges to produce a number of different-height loops. Dowels, rods, and knitting needles make excellent gauges and come in many diameters.

You do not have to make a loop at every interval: some areas can be left as flat plain weave to contrast with groups of loops. Do not remove the gauge until you have woven a few rows of plain weave to secure the loops.

The yarn, the sett of the warp, and the desired denseness will determine how many loops to have in a row, and how many rows of plain weave between the rows of pulled loops.

If you are using the same weft yarn alternately for the background and for the pulled loops, the position of the loops can either be staggered or vertical. To change the position of the loops in the next row, weave an odd number of picks. Remember that the loops are not knotted and may pull out if you do not beat them in firmly and secure them by at least one row of plain weave. There should be at least one row of plain weave on either side of a row of loops. You can use 2 weft threads, one for the loops and another for the background. A thick, textured weft might be used for the pattern, and a thin weft as the plain-weave background structure.

The loops look best if they are placed close together and woven firmly. All the loops in a row should twist in the same direction. Remember that the loops progress towards the weft side to allow enough slack for later adjustment, if necessary. The gauge determines the size of the loops, and if a close sett or a heavy yarn is used, the loops will stand up and support each other. The amount of weft needed varies, depending on the size of the loop and the thickness of the weft, but allow at least three times the weaving width of the row.

4-6. Variations on pulled loops, combining different groupings, spacing, and yarns. (Photo: Hector Garcia)

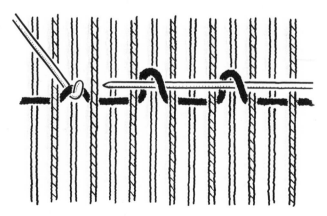

4-7. To form pulled loops, use either your fingers or a crochet hook to lift the weft thread onto a dowel rod or to gauge the diameter of the desired size of the loop.

69

Knotted Piles

There are three traditional rug-weaving knots that should be a major part of the weaving vocabulary: (1) the *Senna*, or Persian, knot; (2) the *Ghiordes*, or Turkish, knot, which has identical counterparts in the Scandinavin *rya* and *flossa* knots; and (3) the *Spanish* knot. Each of these knots can be made from a continuous weft yarn that is wound off a bobbin or butterfly. The loops can be cut, left uncut, or a combination of the two. The loops can also be effective if they vary in height. If you insert precut lengths of weft yarn individually, you will have complete control over the number of strands in a knot, the number of knots, and the color, texture, length, and placement of each knot. Knotting is an incredibly free technique with very few restrictions.

The Senna knot is tied over two adjacent warp yarns. The weft-pile yarn passes under one warp and over and around the other. The pile end stands out from the warp threads. The Senna knot can be tied in either a left-hand or a right-hand direction (figure 4-8).

The Ghiordes knot is the most common and the most versatile of the three. The tufts of pile yarn are usually inserted in pairs between 2 warp threads, although the strands in the pile may vary in texture, number, color, and length, depending on the desired effect. You can either cut the yarn into individual lengths and make a fringe or unwind it continuously from a butterfly and make cut or uncut loops . Individual knots allow for more subtle variations and greater control.

To cut the yarn in uniform lengths, make a gauge from a strong piece of cardboard or wood. Wind each color of yarn evenly around the gauge without overlapping and cut along the edge with scissors or a razor blade (figure 4-9). Each color and change in length should be kept separate so that you can use it by itself or in combinations. Several tones of the same color make the pile more brilliant than a single tone. A variety of textures can work beautifully together, but the simplicity of a single type of yarn is also attractive.

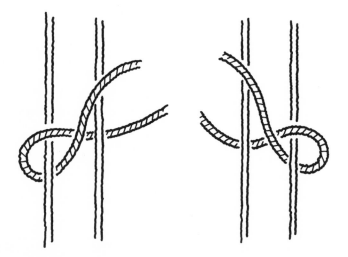

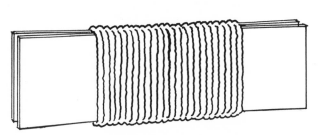

4-8. A Senna knot can be formed in either a left-hand or a right-hand direction. Several rows of plain weave are needed between the rows of knots to reinforce the structure and to hold the pile in place.

4-9 Use a gauge to cut uniform lengths of yarn.

4-10. Jane Redman. Hanging with uncut Ghiordes loops and precut fringe on the bottom row. (Photo: Hector Garcia)

The spacing of the pile may vary; about four knots per inch and 2 threads per knot is standard on the frame loom if there are 8 threads to an inch in the warp. The sett can be changed on the frame loom to fit the diameter and thickness of the yarn. The amount of yarn for each knot should be about two times the desired length of the pile.

There are two ways to make a Ghiordes knot from a precut strand of yarn: (1) Lay a length of cut yarn over 2 warp threads and pass the ends behind and between them (figure 4-11). (2) Pass the length of the yarn under a pair of warp threads (figure 4-12); hold both ends of the yarn together above the warp threads, creating a loop (figure 4-13); divide the pair of warp threads in half (figure 4-14); pass the strands underneath the warp threads and in between them through the center from back to front (figure 4-15). There must be several rows of plain weave in between the rows of knots to hold the pile in place and to make the fabric sturdy (figure 4-16). The plain-weave ground will be covered, so the only requirement is to use a strong yarn.

If you are combining a pile with some other technique that is intended to show, it is important to weave enough of a background so that the pile does not cover parts of the design that are meant to be seen. The placement of the knots should be staggered on every other row to avoid small openings or vertical lines of knots and to make the construction stronger.

After you have made a row of knots according to your design, open the shed, weave the necessary number of rows of plain weave, and beat the weft down.

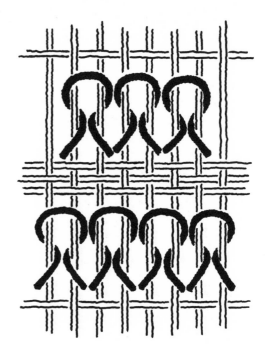

4-11. Precut-pile construction with each strand of weft knotted individually. Two or more yarns may be used for the same knot.

4-12. Pass the precut length of yarn under 2 warp threads. (Photo: Hector Garcia)

4-13. Hold the ends of the weft lengths together above the warp. (Photo: Hector Garcia)

4-14. Either from the left or the right divide the pair of warp threads in half and pull the strand ends to the side. (Photo: Hector Garcia)

4-15. Pull the strand ends through the center of the warp threads. (Photo: Hector Garcia)

4-16. Complete the knot by pulling it down against several rows of plain weave. This method of tying a Ghiordes knot is finished in a few smooth movements, and the precut pile is fairly even. (Photo: Hector Garcia)

To make a Ghiordes knot from a continuous weft, start with a butterfly of the weft or wefts that you are going to use. Before you begin, secure the weft with plain weave. The weft may be woven across the entire row or only for 1/2″, as long as it is secure. You may incorporate the end of the weft into the pile if it blends in by letting the weft end hang down in front of the piece with the pile strands, or you can leave about 1″ to be woven in after the first row of knots is completed. Put the gauge that determines the height of the pile on top of the warp above the last row of plain weave. Starting from the left, pass the weft over the gauge; under the left warp; over, around, and under the right warp; and under the gauge (figure 4-17). Pull down to tighten the knot around the two warps, then start the next knot. A continuous weft produces the same knot as the individual strands. Pull each loop just enough to make it even with the other loops. The loop around the gauge forms the looped surface; the loops around the 2 warp threads holds the surface loop in place.

Leave the gauge in place after you have completed a row of knots until you have woven and beaten in several rows (1/4″−1/2″) of plain weave. The weft used for the loops may be woven back in plain weave to return to the starting point, or the loop may be reversed, and the weft begun from the other side after the ground is woven in with another weft.

The same weft may be used for the loops and the plain-weave background in small areas. Large projects need two separate wefts—one for the background, the other for the design.

You can change colors in the same row, leaving the cut ends hanging as part of the pile in front. If the loops are uncut, leave the end hanging in back and weave it in place, or weave it into the design in plain weave. Again, stagger the knots and pack the weaving in tightly.

A continuous weft is used to best advantage if there are fairly large areas of the same color. Ghiordes knots may also be used to secure objects such as sticks in the weaving (figure 4-18). The loops may be cut, uncut, or only sections of loops cut.

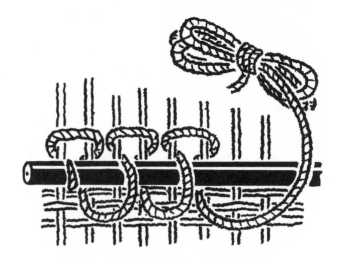

4-17. A Ghiordes knot formed with a continuous weft.

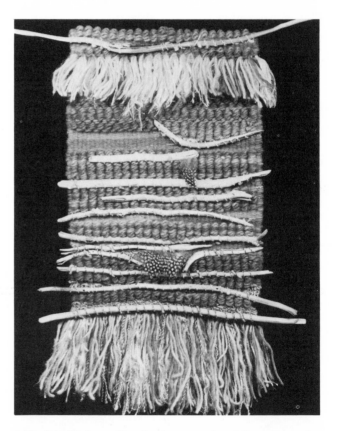

4-18. Jane Redman. Hanging incorporating driftwood into the weave. The wood was used as a gauge for the Ghiordes knots and left in the piece. The knots hold the driftwood securely. (Photo: Hector Garcia)

The Ghiordes knot is the foundation for the Scandinavian rya and flossa knots. The main difference between the two lies in the density and length of the pile. A flossa pile is short and close, and it stands up straight (figure 4-19). Only a few picks of plain weave are woven between the rows of knots, and fine detailing shows clearly. A rya pile is much shaggier, it falls at different angles, and it may have an inch or more of plain weave in between the rows of knots.

Rya and flossa can have loops of the same height or a mixture of heights. They can be used in clusters on a flat tapestry surface. Designs with long rya piles work best when they are bold. Simple geometric patterns are ideal for this technique.

A Spanish knot encircles only 1 warp thread (figure 4-20). It is made by twisting a cut-pile weft yarn over a warp yarn and crossing it behind the warp. The two weft-yarn ends come up to the surface on either side of the warp to form the pile. The knots should be held in place with plain-weave rows. The knots tend to slip out before they are secured with plain weave, and they are easier to work over a gauge.

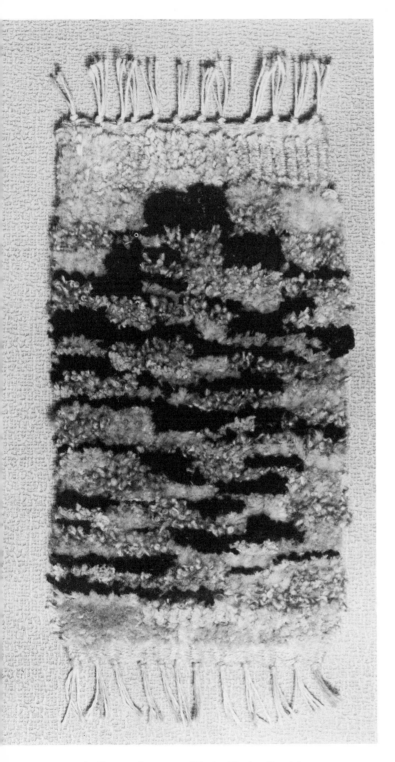

4-19. Flossa pile weave. (Photo: Hector Garcia)

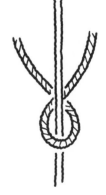

4-20. Spanish knot.

TWINING

Twining techniques evolved even earlier than weaving. They had many versatile applications, from basketry to building a shelter: the walls were formed by twining vines and reeds horizontally into perpendicular poles. Many cultures still use twining to make nets, fabrics, mats, shelters, blankets, and containers. The fibers and materials available help to determine the function that the finished article will fulfill.

Weaving and twining are both formed by interlacing yarns together at right angles. The difference between the two processes is that regular twining employs two wefts at the same time: one weft passes under while the other passes over the warp, and they twist around each other in the space between the warp threads so that the weft which was below the first warp is above the next (figure 4-21). The warp can either be covered or left showing, depending on how closely the twined rows are packed. Twining is a finger-controlled process: no shed is required. The warp is worked flat, and no other equipment, besides a possible comb, is needed.

The continuous twisting and crossing of the two wefts in the same direction produce a horizontal weft that is tight and firm. The weft strands can enclose from 1 to 4 warp threads, depending on the thickness of the strands and the desired effect. The warp is also usually worked in pairs (figure 4-22).

Weft twining can be adapted to patterns ranging from tapestry, in which the wefts are used to build shapes and are confined within specific design areas, to openwork, crocheted and looped piles, and herringbone effects, created by two contrasting colors. The strands can have the same color and texture, or different yarns can be twisted around each other. Seeds, beads, shells, sequins, or other objects can be strung on the wefts and used as decoration just as with the wefts in weaving. Varying effects can be achieved by twisting the wefts clockwise or counterclockwise, changing the order of the colors, and selecting different warp threads.

Twining produces a sturdy fabric. It is a strong, compact structure. As a heading and border for a weaving project it makes a very handsome finish. On a frame loom it helps to space and flatten the warp, hold it in place, and give the first rows of weaving a firm foundation to work from. Twining can proceed in any direction on the frame loom. Since twining does not require a shed, the nail frame loom is most suitable.

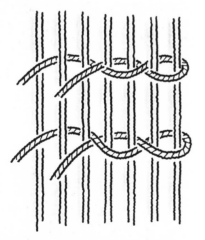

4-21. Twining with 2 warp threads and 2 weft threads. One weft passes over, the other under the warp threads, then the order is reversed, the weft thread on top passing under the next 2 warp threads, and the weft thread on the bottom over the next 2 warp threads. The wefts will twist together automatically.

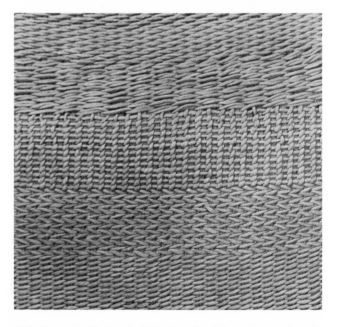

4-22. Susan Dobinsky. Twining sampler. (Photo: Hector Garcia)

CHAINING

The chain stitch is the same as a crochet chain stitch, except that it is done between a series of secured threads rather than on a single strand. Chaining is similar to twining, except that the warp threads are held in place by crocheted weft loops formed by a single yarn. A crochet hook can be used, but your fingers are just as efficient and even quicker. Chaining should be started with a weft that has been secured in plain weave. It can be unwound from a skein or small ball that is easy to manipulate.

The weft passes underneath the warp from one selvage to the other (figure 4-23). It is then picked up from underneath and brought up to the surface in loops in the space between 2 warp threads. The loop is now above the warp and the weft is pulled up in the next space through it to form the next loop.

When you have finished the last row of chaining, pull the end of the weft through the last loop and draw the loop tight. Secure the end by weaving it back in over and under the last few warp threads. If you have made many rows of chaining, secure the weft by passing it through the last loop, pull it tight, and return in a plain weave to the starting point. In this case the weft is used for both the chain and the plain weave. For pieces that require large quantities of yarn, two separate wefts can be used, one for the chaining and another for the plain weave. Several rows of plain weave between rows of chaining are advisable for large or functional pieces.

Chaining can be worked into shapes and contrasting design areas rather than crossing the entire weaving width. It is usually used to form a tight, controlled surface, but it can also be pulled irregularly to produce a bold, loopy appearance (figure 4-24). Part of the fun and charm of the technique is the ease and freedom that it suggests.

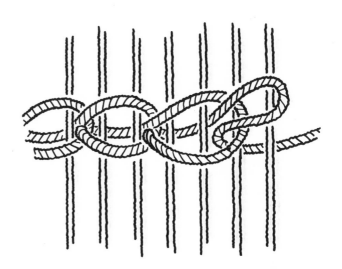

4-23. Chaining may occur between single warp threads or pairs of threads.

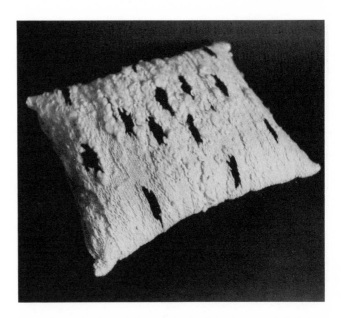

4-24. Susan Feulner. Pillow woven in plain weave and chaining. (Photo: Robert Fields)

Several wefts, colors, textures, or novelty yarns can be chained together in the same row. The number of warp threads to use depends on the thickness of the weft yarns. The effects can be light, airy, loopy, or tightly matted, almost like fleece or fur (figure 4-25). Huge, thick chains can be made for strong, dominant areas in a design. Chaining can look like whipped cream that is put on in thick spirals, or it can be limp and do absolutely nothing. The importance of the interaction of yarn, technique, design, and the desired effect cannot be stressed enough. The right materials, colors, and textures and the technique that brings out their best characteristics is very important. Play with it.

Chain stitches are among the fastest to put in and take out. Children seem to make them one of their favorites. The chain can be moved up and down the warp threads without displacing the tension. It is fun to outline other shapes with rows of chaining. They make a curling, twisting line that has a quality of gaiety.

The amount of yarn used for the chain should be many times the area in which it is being used, since each loop requires a great deal of yarn. There is no set amount that can be specified: different yarns need different amounts, depending on how thick they are, and the tension varies from person to person. It is always a good idea to make a sample before attempting a final project in order to estimate the required yardage.

4-25. Sampler demonstrating the variety of loops and effects that can be achieved with chaining. (Photo: Hector Garcia)

SOUMAK

Soumak is the name of a weaving center in Asia Minor in which the technique generally known as *soumak* was developed. It is a construction with a large range of applications. It has been classed as a rug technique, a tapestry and embroidery technique (stem stitch), and a pile weave.

The basic structure consists of a weft thread that passes over the top of a warp thread, under it, and then over it again. The warp thread is encircled automatically (figure 4-26). The weft yarn may wrap around a single warp thread or a group of warp threads in a variety of patterns. It is often used as an outline for tapestry (figures 4-27 and 4-28). Contrasting shapes can be formed in small areas with soumak as with tapestry (figure 4-29). Or soumak may be worked in rows across the entire width of the warp (figure 4-30).

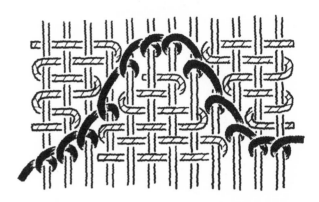

4-27. Outlining plain-weave tapestry shapes with soumak.

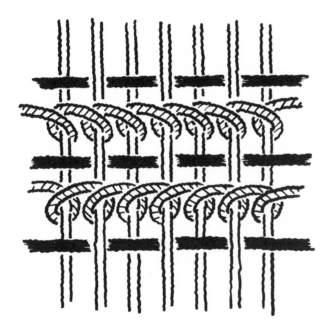

4-26. Single soumak interspersed with rows of plain weave.

4-28. Nancy Sullivan. Hanging incorporating soumak as an outlining technique. The soumak produces a secondary textural pattern. (Photo: Hector Garcia)

4-29. Contrasting shapes formed by combining soumak with tapestry. (Courtesy of Sharon Shattan)

4-30. Marian Konrad. Soumak design. (Courtesy of the artist)

Soumak may be handled in many ways. You can use two wefts, one for the soumak pattern and another finer one as a binding plain-weave tabby. If plain weave is used across the entire weaving width, it automatically closes the slits that occur if a line of soumak has been interrupted by the introduction of new colors or shapes.

In small areas the same yarn that is used for the soumak may be used for the plain weave. To keep directions with a single yarn, first work in a row of soumak, then weave in an odd row of plain weave so that the yarn is back at the starting point. To reverse direction, weave in an even number of rows of plain weave so that the weft yarn ends up at the opposite side to the starting point, or simply reverse the direction of the soumak after the first row. If soumak stitches are worked in the same direction, they will all be on the same slant. If the direction is reversed, the result is a knitted or herringbone appearance.

Rows of plain weave between the rows of soumak add firmness, especially for functional articles such as rugs, purses, or pillows. If you use a finer weft for the plain-weave tabby than for the soumak, it will not be visible between the rows of soumak.

If a row of soumak is worked across the entire weaving width and followed by a row of plain weave in a different weft, the next row of soumak reverses automatically. To keep the slant of the soumak weft in the same direction, it must either be cut and started again on the original side or woven back to the starting point in plain weave.

There are several variations of soumak. The most elaborate is *Greek soumak*, in which the weft yarn is wrapped three or more times around a single warp thread before moving on to the next warp (figure 4-31). The weft yarn is unwound from a bobbin or butterfly. Greek soumak is worked on a flat surface and does not need a shed. Plain weave may be used in alternate rows to produce a ribbed effect, or the soumak may be used by itself (figure 4-32). Greek soumak is worked from the top side, facing the weaver, and from either the left or the right, depending on the direction of the warping. The knot may be pulled down very tight for a close weave or left loosely on a widely spaced warp to produce a lacy effect (figure 4-33).

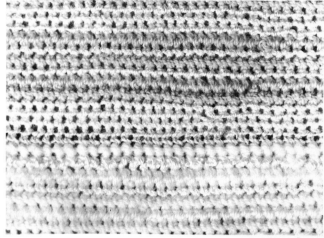

The classic method is *oriental soumak*, in which the weft yarn passes over 4 warp threads and back under 2, although any other combination can also be used (figure 4-34).

4-31. Greek soumak. The weft encircles a warp thread three or more times.

4-32. *Wind Shield*. Sherry Boemmel. Greek soumak. The thick, uneven texture of the yarn enhances the construction in an untraditional way. (Photo: Hector Garcia)

4-33. Greek soumak in a variety of weft yarns. (Photo: Hector Garcia)

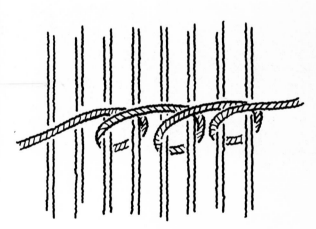

4-34. Oriental soumak.

C-1. Weaving materials come in a vast range of colors, weights, and textures that are exciting to touch as well as to look at. Each yarn has its own character and personality. See page 32 on yarns. (Yarns courtesy of Fibre and Form; photo: Robert Fields)

C-2. Jane Redman. Double-layer weave. The two warps are interchanged with each other, and the synthetic bouclé threads are left floating on the top layer, attached to the bottom warp in a few places. See page 37 on warps that show in the weave. (Photo: Hector Garcia)

C-3. *Color.* Virginia Virak. Hanging in a combination of techniques: plain weave, tapestry, soumak, and Egyptian knots. See page 46 on yarn colors. (Photo: Hector Garcia)

C-4. Double-layer hanging woven in tapestry with Egyptian knots. See page 92 on double weaves. (Courtesy of Sharon Shattan; photo: Hector Garcia)

C-5. *Color Kite.* Nancy Sullivan. See page 126 on shape. (Photo: Hector Garcia)

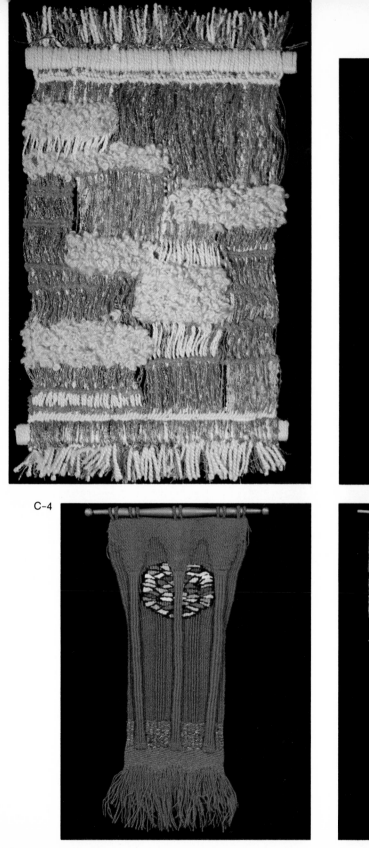

C–2

C–3

C–4

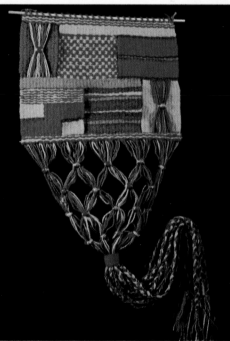

C–5

83

Another method, *single soumak*, is also referred to as Swedish knotting, depending on which side will be seen in the finished piece (figures 4-35 and 4-36). Only 1 warp thread is wrapped at a time. The design is worked with the "wrong" side up for a Swedish knot; the "right" side, with the single soumak, will appear as dashes composed of slanting lines that have a twill effect. The Swedish knot will appear ribbed and wrapped, producing a strong vertical coil (figure 4-37). To avoid a slit while changing colors, interloop the adjoining wefts. First make a beginning knot with the new weft on the next warp. With a tapestry needle tuck the end of the first weft down through the new weft and pull the end parallel to the warp.

An *Egyptian knot* completely encircles each warp thread to produce a corded effect (figure 4-38). It is similar to the Swedish knot in appearance, but the work is done with the right side—the side that will be seen—facing the weaver. This is an advantage in combining Egyptian knots with other techniques. The knot is worked in alternate directions, but the change in direction does not show. To make changes in color or shape, tie the yarn in a slip knot and tuck in the end on the underside, or pull the tail of the yarn down inside the rib with a tapestry needle.

The weft yarn is wound in a continuous line from the butterfly, and it takes several rows for the beauty of the technique to show. To make an Egyptian knot in a left-to-right direction, pass the weft yarn under the warp, up and over the warp to the left, and down under the warp to the right (figure 4-39). Pull the weft yarn down, tighten, and move on consecutively to the next warp. The next row changes direction, so the knot is reversed. The weft passes under the warp from the right, over the warp to the right, and down under the warp to the left (figure 4-40).

The Egyptian knot does not require plain weave in between the rows of knots, but it may be used effectively in combination with plain-weave tapestry (figure 4-41).

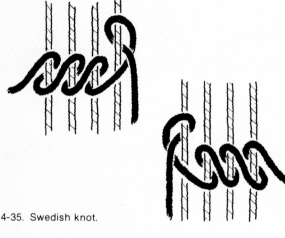

4-35. Swedish knot.

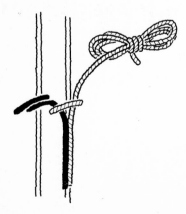

4-36. Joining two colors in a Swedish knot.

4-37. Sampler of Swedish knots. (Photo: Hector Garcia)

84

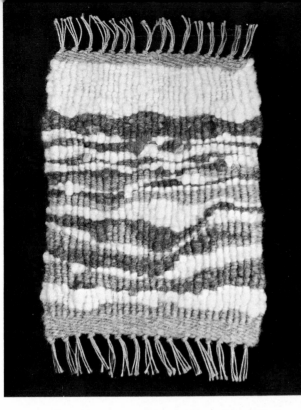

4-38. The Egyptian knot produces a strong ribbed effect similar to the Swedish knot. (Photo: Hector Garcia)

4-39. Left-to-right Egyptian knot.

4-40. Right-to-left Egyptian knot.

4-41. *Inside*. Jane Redman. Wall hanging in plain weave and Egyptian knots, hung at a 90° angle, 27″ × 38″. The heavy nubs are formed with Egyptian knots. The yarn is a handspun thick-and-thin novelty yarn. (Photo: Hector Garcia)

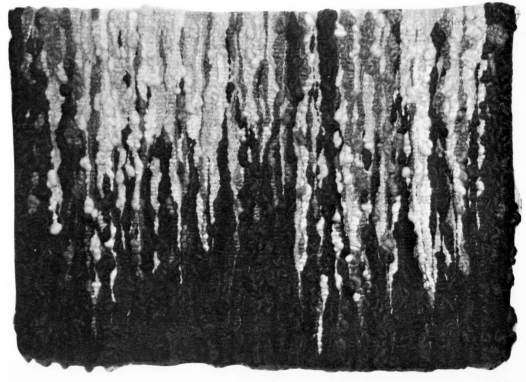

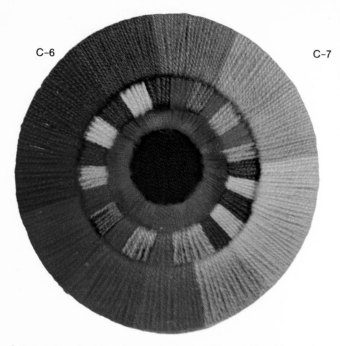

C-6. A color wheel is only representative of the relationships and harmonies between hues. The inner circles are composed of complementary-color schemes and a collection of reds in a variety of yarns, respectively. See page 40 on the color wheel. (Photo: Hector Garcia)

C-8

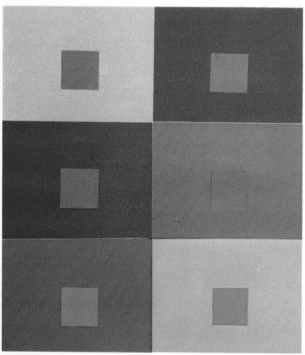

C-7. Color blanket in plain weave. A study of how the same weft appears in combination with different colors is the best way to understand and control color relationships. See page 43 on color blankets. (Photo: Hector Garcia)

C-8. Place a square of a secondary color on a primary-color background and observe what happens. There may be not only a change in the value but also a definite change in the color itself. The primary color subtracts its hue from the secondary color. See page 42 on color relationships. (Photo: Hector Garcia)

C-9. *Outward.* Jane Redman. Tapestry weave based on hachures. Flamelike shapes are repeated and interlock like fingers. See page 62 on hachures. (Photo: Hector Garcia)

C-10. Jane Redman. Pile weave with a combination of materials that are cut and shaped in different lengths. See page 70 on cutting yarns. (Photo: Hector Garcia)

C-11 and C-12 captions on page 90.

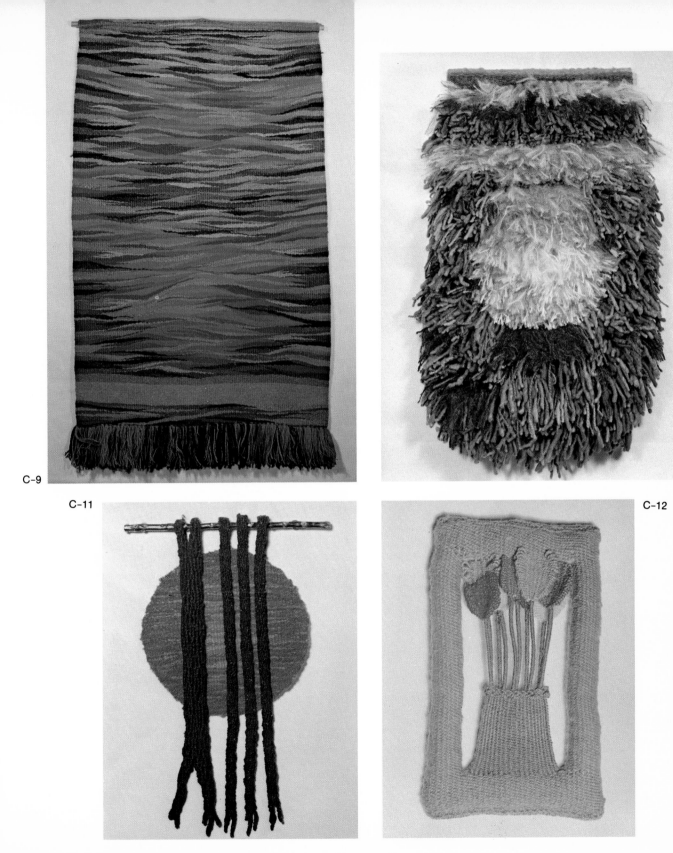

C-9

C-10

C-11

C-12

WRAPPING

Wrapping is a technique in which the weft simply spirals around the warp. The weft is either tied and pulled inside with a needle or continues in the weaving (figure 4-42). Wrapping combined with plain weave or tapestry produces fascinating results (figures 4-43 and 4-44). Single warp threads (figure 4-45) or groups of 3 or 4 threads may be wrapped in a variety of combinations to produce a branch-like pattern.

Long strands of pile may be partially or completely wrapped, with only tufts showing at the ends. An entire piece done in wrapping is under such great tension that when it is released from the loom, the wrapped warps will curl. If this is not desirable, the piece may be stretched and mounted on a board or backing for support.

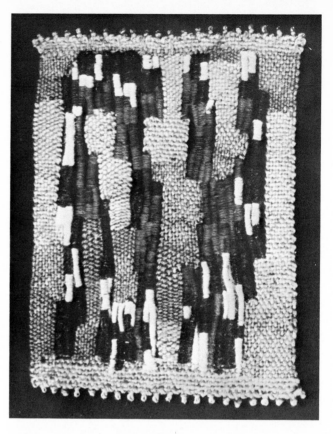

4-43 and 4-44. Tina Kyrthe. Plain weave and wrapping (full piece and detail). (Courtesy of the artist)

4-42. Wrapping is most effective with a smooth yarn and even spiraling. The ends may either be pulled down inside the wrapped warp thread or continued in the weaving. (Photo: Hector Garcia)

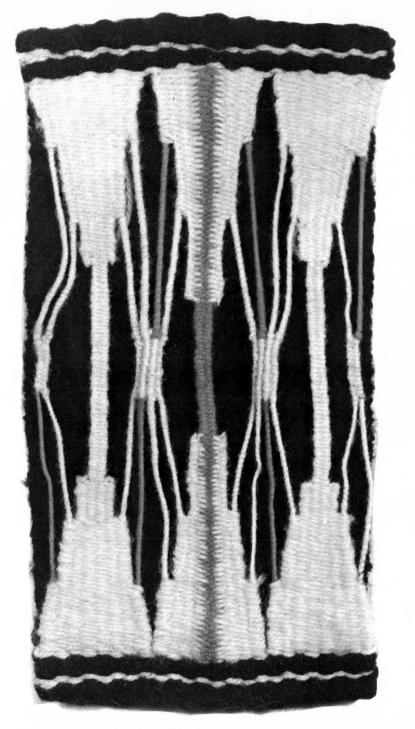

4-45. Odette Brabec. Wrapped single warp threads combined with tapestry weave in a double layer. (Photo: Hector Garcia)

See page 87.

C-11. Marilyn Ruck. Hanging with a tapestry-woven circle and Egyptian knots. See page 84 on Egyptian knots. (Photo: Hector Garcia)

C-12. *Tulips.* Hazel Pensock. Tubular double weave, wrapping, and tapestry weave. See page 100 on tubular weave. (Photo: Hector Garcia)

C-13. Ing Marie Lutz. Detail of a sampler showing a variety of weights of yarn and changes in sett. Precut pile fringes are braided and otherwise manipulated on the surface. See page 37 on weft yarns. (Photo: Robert Fields)

C-14. *Trees.* Joyce Richards. Wrapping and tapestry weave. See page 88 on wrapping. (Courtesy of the artist)

C-15. *Earth I.* Jane Redman. Tapestry weave, Egyptian knots, and soumak, 36″ × 40″. The surface texture is created by the combination of woven constructions and materials. See also figures 1–46 and 1–47. (Photo: Hector Garcia)

C-16. Small sample woven with gold packaging cord and metallic threads in a tapestry weave. See page 34 on novelty yarns. (Photo: Hector Garcia)

C-14

C-15

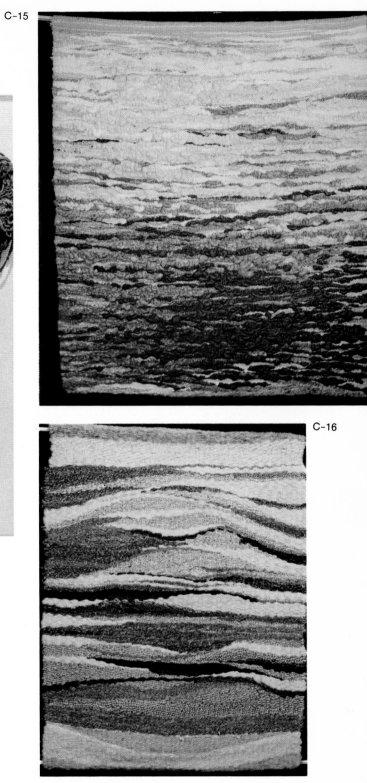

C-16

DOUBLE WEAVES

Double-woven constructions are formed by two layers of fabric, one woven on top of the other. The layers may either be joined or separate (figure 4-46). Both layers are woven simultaneously on a hand-loom and are interdependent. Each layer requires two harnesses when it is woven in plain weave. The warp and the weft both show in traditional double cloth.

The Frame Loom

The simple nail frame loom is very versatile, and the concept of multiple layers is easily adapted from the handloom, in which harnesses control the selection of warp threads and sheds, to the frame loom, in which the fingers manipulate the layers. The two layers are wound on the loom as one warp and then separated and treated as two different warps.

Depending on the purpose, the fabric can be woven as two separate layers; in tubular form, with the two layers connected on both the top and bottom edges of each side; or in tubular sections (figure 4-47). The nail frame loom adapts the principles of double weave very freely and allows for innovative departures such as adding extra layers after the weaving has been started or weaving more than two layers in a few areas (figure 4-48). Different setts and weights of yarns may be mixed. Once you have understood the concept and the implications of multilayers, the design possibilities and structural innovations become almost limitless.

Both layers do not have to progress simultaneously, and they can be woven not only in contrasting colors but in different techniques. The layers can be joined at any point; they can be woven as a single layer in some areas and double in others. Sections or an entire piece can be woven into tubular shapes. There are many dimensional and sculptural possibilities to be explored. The weaver has access to both sides and both layers without interlocking the two warps: the loom can simply be turned over to work on the opposite layer. Or, if the loom is large, you may invent some support system, stand the loom upright, and walk around it in order to have access to both layers of the weaving.

4-46. *Yellow Forests.* Ruth Ginsberg. (Courtesy of the Art Institute of Chicago)

4-47. Joyce Richards. Tubular-weave sculpture.
(Photo: Robert Fields)

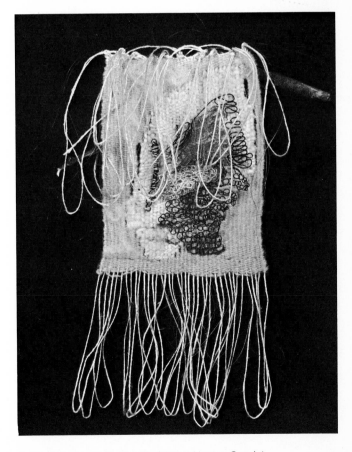

4-48. *Cocoon.* Betty Bondi. (Photo: Hector Garcia)

C-17. *Lion-Mask.* Bonnie Kondor. The background is plain-weave tapestry, and the design is pile weave and wrapping. See page 67 on pile weaves. (Photo: Robert Fields)

C-18. Pattern based on diagonal slits and triangular shapes. The jagged rhythm and the zigzag movement are established by repeating the lightning-bolt shapes in different colors and widths. See page 55 on diagonal slits. (Courtesy of Gwynne Lott)

C-19. *Hive.* Marilyn Ruck. See page 115 on decorative edges. (Photo: Hector Garcia)

C-20. *Bugs.* Sue Feulner. Tubular double weave with rya. See page 100 on tubular weave. (Photo: Robert Fields)

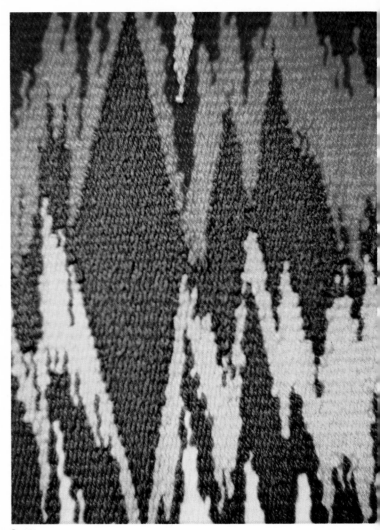

C-18

C-19

C-20

Warping

The colors of the warp do not have to be taken into account unless they are intended to show as part of the design or to be left unwoven. The most suitable techniques for double layers on a frame loom are tapestry, knotted constructions, pile weaves, wrapped warps, and even delicate lace weaves or open lacelike effects (figure 4-49). A lace weave can be very effective against a tapestry background (figure 4-50). Macramé is sometimes effective as a double layer (figure 4-51). The warp threads act as filler threads, and the wrapping threads are 2 strands of precut pile. The precut pile is knotted on 2 warp threads, and the direction of the loom is reversed so that the weaver is working down the warp threads. A square knot (figures 4-52 and 4-53) works well for the macramé, as does a half-knot, which is formed by always coming from either the right (clockwise spiral) or the left (counterclockwise spiral) and never changing direction. The ends of the strands are either used in the weaving or pulled inside a rib or the core of the macramé sennit.

As mentioned in Chapter 1, the nail frame loom may be warped in a sett of 4, 8, 10, 12, or 16 threads to the inch. A very close sett of 16 or more threads per inch would be much too tedious to manipulate by hand, but one warp may be very close and fine, while the other is coarser and more widely spaced.

Several methods may be used to prepare the loom for double layers, depending on which yarns and techniques are going to be used. The warp may be wound on the loom in a sett of 8 threads to the inch and then divided into separate warps, each with 4 threads to the inch. Each warp may then be woven in a tapestry technique independently of the other warp.

Two separate warps with totally different yarns and setts may be wound on the frame. Put one warp on the loom, then the next layer. If both warps follow the same path, it is advisable to use two distinctive colors, one for each warp. Two or more warps may be used on the frame loom in any combination of colors, textures, or threads per inch, depending on the weave, the construction, and the intention of the weaver.

4-49. Susan Feulner. Tubular-weave sections enclosing a stuffed tubular-weave form woven in rya. (Photo: Hector Garcia)

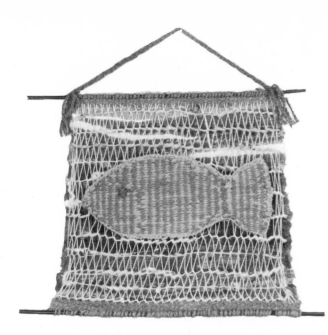

4-50. *Fish in a Net*. Dorothy Magos. Lace weave combined with tapestry weave. (Photo: Robert Fields)

4-52 and 4-53. Square knot, crossing over the filler threads from the left, then from the right.

4-51. Macramé is easily incorporated into a weaving on the frame loom. Simply turn the loom upside down and macramé, using the warp threads as filler threads and a precut strand, several times the desired length, as wrapping threads. (Photo: Hector Garcia)

Weaving

The concept involved in double layers is relatively simple. If the layers are intended to fit together, they are woven together by combining the warp threads from one layer with the corresponding warp threads from the other layer. The sequence and the number of threads is dependent on the weave: a plain weave, for example, would combine 1 warp thread from each layer if the warps were equally distributed. If the warp threads in the various layers are not equal, a ratio must be worked out. If you have two warps, for example, one with 8 threads to the inch and the other with 4 threads to the inch, they can be balanced by combining 2 threads from one layer with 1 thread from the other. The warps must be combined at some point—either at the top and bottom of the piece or at change points in the weaving—or you will have two separate pieces when you cut the project off the loom.

To start, weave in the tension sticks with a plain weave that combines both layers. The heading may be woven in the same way to connect the layers, even though the layers may be connected to each other at any other point in the weaving. Techniques such as soumak, twining, chaining, and Egyptian knots are very useful constructions for connecting the layers. Once you have woven in the tension sticks and the heading, you are ready to begin the actual weaving.

Every thread in the top layer must be raised and separated from the other warp threads. Insert a piece of paper or cardboard between the two layers. it should be the width of the project and at least a few inches high. This helps to distinguish the two layers of warp threads from each other. After you have woven several inches, the layers tend to separate and the distinction becomes obvious. The insert may then be removed or left in to aid your concentration (figure 4-54). It can be helpful if the colors and textures of the design in one layer confuse the visual effects in the other layer. The insert must be removed occasionally to view the total effect of both layers.

After the warps are divided, they are handled as structurally separate parts of the design. Turn the frame loom over when you want to look at the opposite layer (figure 4-55).

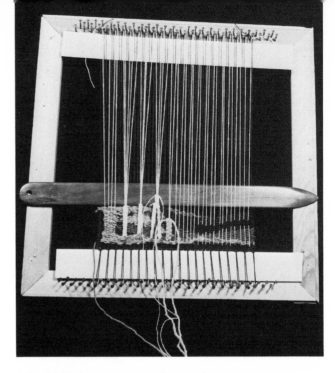

4-54. Divided warp prepared for weaving in two layers. Separate warps in different setts are easier to distinguish if the warps are in different colors. (Photo: Hector Garcia)

4-55. To gain access to the bottom warp, turn the loom over. The layers are connected by pulling one layer of warp threads up between the other layer of warp threads. When the weft is woven through both layers, the warps interlock, i.e., the layers are interchangeable. (Photo: Hector Garcia)

Adding Extra Layers

Extra warp threads may be added onto a woven surface after a project has already been started (figure 4-56). The easiest method is to take a long strand of yarn and attach it in a rug knot, such as rya. Cut a strand the desired length plus a few inches and knot it on the warp in the usual manner. Pull the ends of the precut strand toward either end of the frame loom, depending on the placement of the new warp threads, and tie them around the nails, either together or individually.

Other warp threads may be added to the design by simply winding them onto the frame loom around the top and bottom nails over what has previously been woven. The new warp can be included with the other warps at the very top and bottom.

Another method of adding warp threads is to pull each new thread down through the ribs—if the project is in a tapestry technique—and out towards the top and bottom stretchers. Pull the additional warp threads in both directions and fasten them securely around the nails with a firm knot. Depending on how many threads are added in this manner, it is possible to use a tapestry needle and, instead of tying each thread individually, to warp the loom in the usual way by passing the thread around the nail. The only difference is that the warp must pass through the woven tapestry rib before it passes around the corresponding nail on the other stretcher.

If you are adding only a few warp threads, it is not necessary to secure them at both ends. It is sufficient to secure the new warp by pulling the tail end inside the rib for at least 2". Multiple layers may easily be superimposed on top of each other. All of the layers do not have to extend across the entire weaving width: some sections may be double or triple, and other areas may be single. Experiment to find the right solution for each problem. These suggestions are only given as guidelines. Make sure, however, that whatever you do is firm and secure.

4-56. Methods of adding extra warp threads. From left to right: a precut pile knot such as rya; winding another warp over what has already been woven; pulling a new warp thread down into the tapestry ribs. (Photo: Hector Garcia)

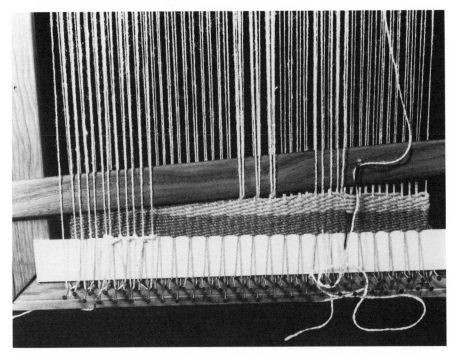

Tubular Weave

In a tubular double weave the top and bottom layers are woven alternately. The weft is woven across the top layer, then the loom is turned over, and the weft continues across the bottom layer. The loom is turned over again to position the weft at the starting point. As a result the weft encircles both warps, and each edge of the top and bottom layers is connected (figure 4-57). The process is simple and can be used for purses, bags, pillowcases, toys, or sculptural pieces (figure 4-58). It has many diverse applications but works best on a frame loom with weft-faced techniques.

All the knotting techniques described earlier work beautifully, since each consecutive warp thread is encircled. The weft moves continuously around the layers in the same direction. When the butterfly is finished, pull the end of the yarn down inside the rib or leave it inside the tube. Secure the next thread and start where the last one finished. Allow for extra width, since stuffing will pull the sides in slightly—like putting a pillow in a pillowcase. A tubular weave has no seams, since it is one continuous weft.

If you are designing a project in a tubular plain weave, consider using an odd number of warp threads in order to avoid double threads at the edges.

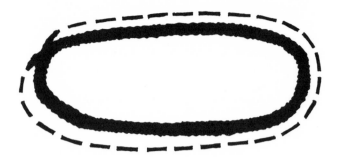

4-57. Tubular double weave.

4-58. Chris Portoghese. Doll, shaped on the loom in tubular double weave. (Photo: Hector Garcia)

The layers can be joined at the bottom, separated later, and joined again. The tubes can even be stuffed and joined as the weaving progresses. To make a purse, for example, weave the layers together at the bottom, divide the warp, and weave a tubular shape (figure 4-59). To make the flap, weave only one layer and leave the top threads floating. After you remove the piece from the loom, the threads can be cut and pulled down into adjacent ribs with a tapestry needle. It is advisable to use a warp that is approximately the same color as the weft in order to avoid a spotty edge.

Sections of a warp can be selected and woven in a tubular form. Single layers might be contrasted with tubular or double layers. The frame loom does not have to be prepared in advance for a double weave done in a tapestry technique, but there must be at least 4 threads to the inch in each layer.

Any pictorial design can be woven in a tubular form as long as the sides at the edge of the layers are joined. If you are working with many shapes, two butterflies, one for each side, can be used to join the edges, while separate wefts are used for the design. An interlocking method such as dovetailing might be necessary for practical items that will be used and worn.

4-59. Marilyn Ruck. Tubular-weave purse. (Photo: Robert Fields)

LACE WEAVES

Finger-controlled, weaver-manipulated lace weaves offer a totally different approach to designing on the frame loom as far as the possible effects and potentials are concerned. The lace weaves should be part of the weaver's vocabulary (figure 4-60).

Plain weave can be manipulated to produce intricate-looking lacy patterns rather than the more solid appearance of tapestry. Warp threads can be tied, wrapped, interlocked, braided, or woven into open-air ethereal shapes and figures that are interrupted by intervals of space.

The lace weaves can be used in conjunction with tapestry or double weave or by themselves as a single layer of bands and areas of lace (figure 4-61). The warp might be woven in blocks and divisions of lace and contrasted with solid areas.

A wider sett of 8 threads to the inch on the nail frame loom will change the appearance of the weave. Sometimes the lace weaves are adapted to resemble tapestry. It is interesting to try the structures on a traditional warp that is spaced closely—for example, 12 threads to the inch—and then on a wider-spaced warp. The frame can also be warped with different setts in different areas. The warp can vary in bands across the weaving width to produce different weaves and effects. Solid areas can be contrasted with open, weblike areas. If the colors and textures of the warp and weft are both to show, use interesting yarns with character such as a bouclé, looped, rough, or nubbed yarn (figure 4-62).

Spanish lace, or *eyelet*, is another adaptation of plain weave (figure 4-63). One weft yarn is used, which may or may not cover the warp, depending on the desired effect. The weft is carried from one side to the other by a needle, butterfly, bobbin, or small shuttle and woven back and forth within a selected group of warp threads. The choice is completely arbitrary—4, 8, 12—determined by the pattern the weaver prefers. The weft is woven for as many picks as desired, then it moves to the next group of threads.

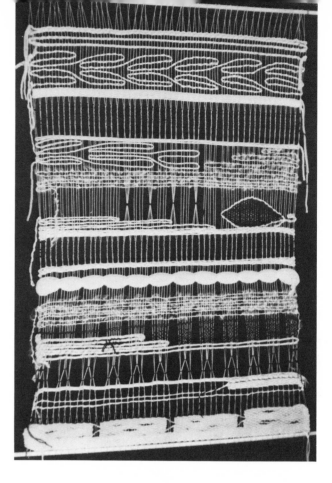

4-61. Dorothy Magos. Tapestry and lace-weave bouquets combined in a double weave. (Photo: Robert Fields)

102

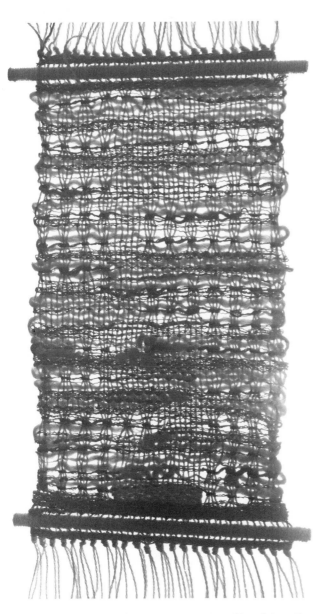

4-62. When both warp and weft show, a yarn with an interesting texture is attractive. (Photo: Hector Garcia)

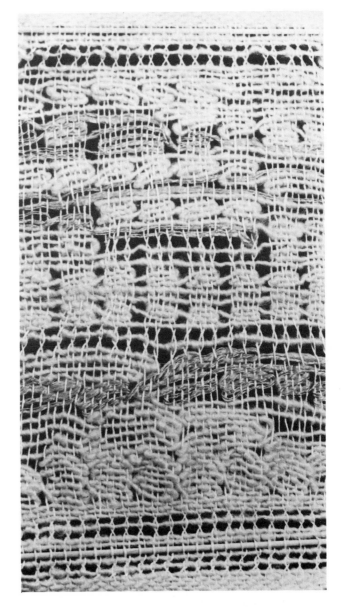

4-63. Sampler showing variations on Spanish lace, or eyelet. (Photo: Hector Garcia)

The next group is woven in the same pattern as the first, and the weft continues until all the groups are woven across the entire weaving width or within the design area (figure 4-64). When the weft returns from the opposite side, the groups can be repeated in the same order. The pattern can be varied by selecting a different number of warp threads in a group, alternating the groups, or changing the number of picks in the weft (figure 4-65).

A *Danish medallion* is woven with 2 contrasting weft threads in a plain weave (figure 4-66). The medallions follow a few rows of weaving. Open the first shed and weave in a heavy weft of a different-color or -texture yarn from left to right. Weave in several picks of a finer or contrasting yarn as high as the medallion is intended to be. The heavier outlining weft travels along the side of the selvage and enters from the right in the opposite shed. Weave it up to the point at which the first medallion is to be placed, stop, and bring the thread out of the shed. With a crochet hook or your finger bring a loop of the heavier yarn over the plain weave and under the first heavy weft. Pass the heavy outlining thread through the loop and pull tightly. This forms the first medallion knot. Continue passing the weft through the shed for the length of the medallion and repeat the process. Continue forming medallions with the weft until it reaches the other side of the warp or the end of the design area. The heavy weft returns in the opposite shed to the right and remains hanging until the next rows of plain weave have been woven. Then the outlining thread is picked up again, and the process is repeated.

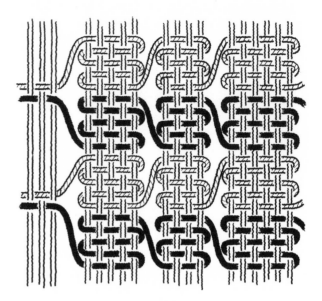

4-64. Regular groups of Spanish lace.

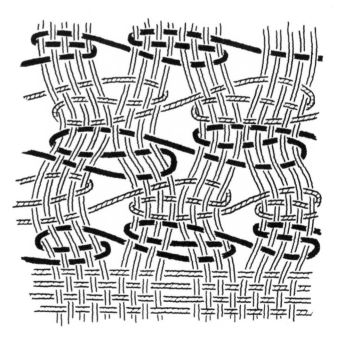

4-65. Irregular groups of Spanish lace.

The medallions are flexible and can be placed freely in a piece (figure 4-67). Size is subject to individual judgment. You can use as many medallions as the design calls for, and they can be placed as high as is structurally feasible. The medallions are usually used to form long, lacy ovals. If they are used for a delicate, lacy effect in a large weaving with a close, fine warp, a harness loom is practical. A nail frame loom might be used for small pieces or for isolated areas broken up into medallions.

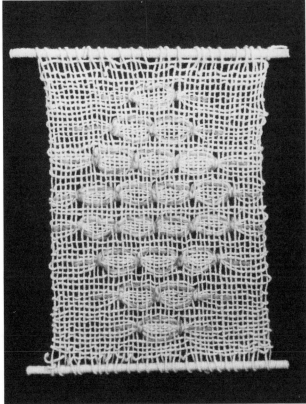

4-67. Design with Danish medallions. (Courtesy of Sharon Shattan)

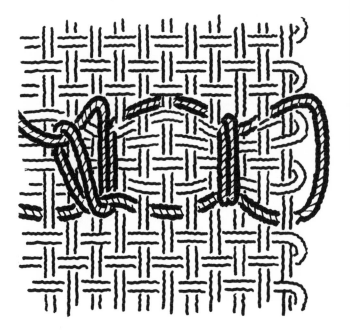

4-66. Danish medallion.

Medallions may be adapted to tapestry, in which case they are not open but appear bricklike (figure 4-68). They cover the warp, and two rows of the outlining weft are needed to make a solid line before forming the medallion. The threads are not pulled tight, but this adaptation is still handsome. The knots can be used as loops to hold thin rods, wood, metal, branches, feathers, or any other decoration. A bead might be threaded on the weft and popped into the center of each medallion. Plain-weave bands and blocks and other weaves can be interspersed in varying proportions and positions throughout the weaving.

Tying groups of warp threads into patterns is probably one of the earliest lace-making techniques. These groups are referred to as *bouquets* (figure 4-69). The warp threads are pulled together by the weft, which encircles the group from front to back and passes through the loop that is formed. At least 3 or 4 warp threads should be used. The groups can be varied in number and size, split apart, and brought together again to form many intricate patterns (figure 4-70). A few rows of plain weave on both sides of the groups help to keep the selvages from pulling in and contribute to the design.

Rows of tied, grouped warp threads are effective in a double weave in which a layer is woven solid behind another open layer. A single layer is divided into two warps, which are handled differently, then woven together with the same weft in the same shed. The warp shows, so it should be a suitable color and texture.

Wrapped threads, unwoven floating threads, slits, or loosely woven plain weave can be used effectively to form an open structure (figure 4-71). Delicate threads that are simply left unwoven in areas will produce a lacy effect. Weaving can also resemble drawnwork: either the warp or the weft or both can be pulled out of the fabric to create openings, and the solid areas connected with embroidery stitches.

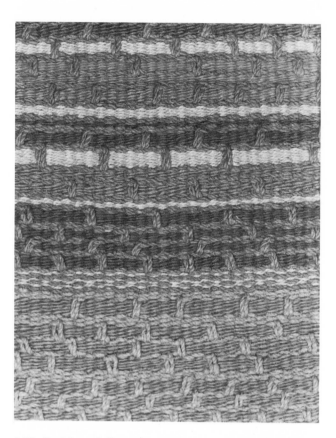

4-68. Danish medallions on a tapestry warp. The weft covers the warp, producing a heavier-looking, bricklike fabric. (Photo: Hector Garcia)

4-69. Jane Redman. Lace hanging with bouquets. (Photo: Edward Miller)

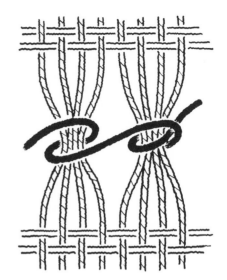

4-70. Bouquets are formed either by gathering groups of warp threads together or by a simple loop pulled tight.

4-71. Sharon Shattan. An open latticework effect can be created in tapestry by weaving slits. The staggered rows create a strong pattern. (Photo: Hector Garcia)

LENO

Warp threads can be twisted around each other and crossed over during weaving to form openwork fabrics. If the crossing is a half twist, the process is referred to as *gauze weaving*, or *leno* (figure 4-72). The complexity or simplicity of the pattern is dependent upon the number and the arrangement of warp threads involved in each crossing (figure 4-73).

With time and patience the leno weaves are possible on every loom. On the nail frame loom the warp threads are picked up and crossed by hand and then slipped onto the pickup stick, which holds the shed open when it is turned on its edges. Then the weft passes through the open shed. The stick is removed, and the weft is beaten carefully. Avoid pulling the weft too tight. The threads will still be twisted in the next row. If you are working on a nail frame loom, slide your finger down the warp from the nail to straighten out the threads. As the threads are untwisted, slip them onto a pickup stick until the weft passes through the shed again. The threads can be twisted in groups of 2, 3, 4, etc., divided, connected, woven alternately with bands of plain weave, or simply formed into blocks and shapes.

INLAY WEAVING

Laid-in, or *inlay*, *weaving* resembles embroidery, but it is done while the weaving is in progress, not after the fabric is finished (figure 4-74). The inlay weaves are a form of brocading, but no extra harnesses or accessory heddles are needed on the loom. Inlays are woven in plain weave and easily adapted to the frame loom. A heddle frame works best for larger projects: the nail frame becomes too tedious for anything larger than small, isolated areas.

The process is simple. A pattern thread is *laid in* the same shed as the background thread (figure 4-75). The technique is similar to tapestry, since the heavy pattern-weft thread moves back and forth only within its own design area. The finer background-weft thread travels across the entire weaving width from selvage to selvage. The weft and the warp that form the background are usually the same color, texture, and weight, although they may be varied.

Weave the background weft across the warp first, then lay in the pattern threads. The pattern wefts do not have to be placed across the entire weaving width: areas of open, sheer space can be contrasted with areas of opaque shapes, as in Swedish h.v. inlay. The inlay technique progresses in a horizontal line, and one shape is not developed before another. Geometric shapes made from triangles, squares, and rectangles are easy to plan and control. Contrasting textures work well together. Do not use a slippery thread for the background warp and weft. The thread should have a tendency to cling so that the weft does not slide out of position. The weft will be somewhat distorted by the displacement of the heavier pattern weft. Try to balance the distribution of the pattern wefts if they are not being woven across the entire piece so that no one side or area becomes lopsided or heavier than another.

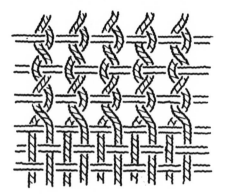

4-72. Leno, or gauze weave.

4-73. Leno sampler being woven on a nail frame loom. The first twist is held in place with the sword until the weft is passed through the shed. The second twist is formed by moving the first twist down from the top of the stretcher. (Photo: Hector Garcia)

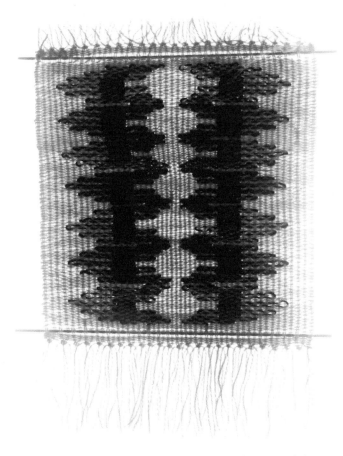

4-74. Nancy Sullivan. Hanging in h.v., or half-tapestry, inlay. (Photo: Hector Garcia)

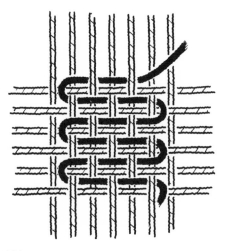

4-75. Laid-in weave.

You can use a flat shuttle on the frame loom, with heddles for the background thread and a threaded needle or butterflies for every shape and color in the pattern. The butterfly continues until the shape is finished, just as in tapestry. Then cut it off and leave a short end hanging on the back side of the weaving. You can also leave the weft on the front as a splice. The new weft starts over the old weft to blend in with the weaving. This is not possible if the wefts are coarse and awkward, so use a relatively fine thread.

The nail frame loom is mechanically clumsy for large areas of laid-in patterns. The loom should only be used for small areas of laid-in weave that can be manipulated by your fingers. Or you can weave a few rows and use a needle to darn in the pattern.

Inlay weaves vary in effect from light and almost transparent to heavy and opaque. In some construction methods such as the Swedish h.v., or half tapestry, the pattern thread is inlaid only in some areas, not across the entire weaving width. The result is a transparent appearance in the sheer areas in which only fine weft threads have been used and an opaque shape in the areas in which the heavier pattern thread has been laid in. Colors and textures may also be laid in at random. As with all weaves the principle is basic, the applications numerous. The effect depends on the design, the texture, and the choice of materials.

The techniques in this chapter are offered only as a starting point for exploration. The spacing of the warp and the interaction of the weft will affect the woven construction. A design that looks great in a hard, twisted yarn may be totally wrong in a slub or novelty yarn. Yet a particular loop may bring out the beauty of a textured, nubby yarn. The weight of the yarn and the spacing of the warp affect the appearance of the knot. The weaver must constantly experiment in order to see what happens and to learn how to perceive, how to form. It is the only way to gain confidence and to develop the knowledge and intuition necessary to achieve the desired results. Each piece, of course, should be well crafted, but the yarns and the techniques will vary according to the needs of the weaver and of the individual woven piece.

CHAPTER 5.

FINISHING

Although this chapter is the shortest in the book, the finishing of a woven piece is by no means the least important consideration of the weaver. A suitable finish that is compatible with the design and purpose of your project is as important as the design and the weave, even though it may take a few minutes to a few hours to complete. How a woven article is intended to be used, presented, or displayed affects the finishing treatment, and there is the further problem of cleaning to be considered. Whether your weaving is a functional project such as a wall hanging, pillow, or purse or simply an experiment, a lack of concern with detailing and securing the threads firmly can easily ruin an otherwise successful piece.

There are several aspects of finishing to think about: removing the piece from the loom; edging to prevent the weft from raveling; decorative finishes, such as borders, fringes, and hanging rods; functional procedures, such as cleaning and blocking; and presentation. Even experimental pieces should be finished in some manner, either matted with a cardboard frame or kept in a notebook or box for future reference. Each project must be handled individually, depending on where it will be seen, the

environment, and the purpose. All of these factors will help you to decide on an appropriate finish.

Experienced weavers often plan the finish and presentation of a project before they start it. If you have been thinking about an idea for a long time, you can anticipate the results and the technical problems and develop an appropriate presentation that is suitable to the design. One way of displaying a hanging, for example, is to build a frame specifically for the piece and leave the piece stretched on the frame under tension (figure 5-1). Or you can stitch the finished piece to another frame (figure 5-2) or stretch it over a board (figure 5-3). These frames are built, stained, or painted specifically as part of the design and the display. A frame may even be wrapped with yarn. It is up to you to experiment and innovate. The nails, for example, may be small finishing nails or tacks that are driven all the way through the wood after the loom is warped. They can either remain visible as part of the piece, or the weaving can be done wrong side up so that the nails do not protrude or show when the frame is turned over. Instead of using nails, grooves and slits can be filed and sawed into the wood. The warp slides down into them and is held in place.

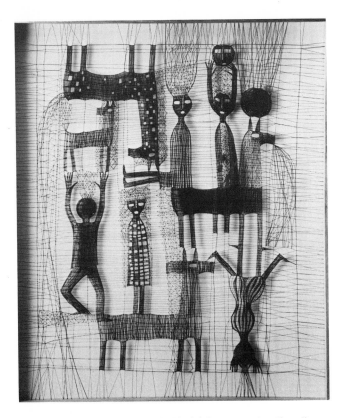

5-1. *Black Comet Dream.* Luba Krejci. Lace construction, linen, Czechoslovakian, 1955, 55″ × 47″. (Courtesy of the Art Institute of Chicago)

5-2. Winifred Bondareff. Tapestry sewn to a frame. (Photo: Robert Fields)

5-3. Josette Lebbin. Tapestry stretched on a board. (Photo: Robert Fields)

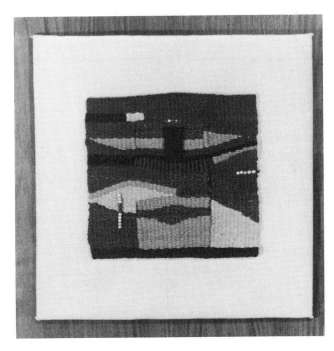

REMOVING THE PIECE FROM THE LOOM
The Nail Frame Loom
The following is the simplest way of removing the weaving from the nail frame loom. Remove the tension sticks from the loom to loosen the warp. There should be at least 1 1/2″ of unwoven warp at both the top and the bottom of the project. Cut the warp threads as close as possible to the nails, starting with the edge that has the most unwoven warp, since it will be easier to knot. Cut a few threads at a time and knot them, preferably with an overhand knot (figure 5-4) so they will hang straight. If the threads are too short or awkward to handle, tie them together with a double knot or a clove-hitch knot (figure 1-22). The disadvantage of the nail frame loom is that the short warp threads fly out in different directions like whiskers. This is no problem if the piece is hemmed and the warp ends are folded under. The only concern is to secure the weft and prevent the threads from raveling.

Knot the warp threads in the same sequence in which they were woven, usually plain weave, although you may have used twining, chaining, Egyptian knots, or soumak for the edge of the heading. Whatever the sequence, it is important to tie together the warp thread that is over the weft and the warp thread that is under the weft in an overhand knot (figure 5-5). If the warp threads were used in pairs, such as the double-layer weaves, then they should be tied in pairs. The same applies to the double basket weave: if the weft pases over 2 threads and under 2 threads, the warp ends should be tied in pairs, which means 4 threads in a group instead of 2.

The Heddle Frame Loom
Removing the finished weaving from a heddle frame loom does not present the same tension problems as the nail frame loom. Since the weaving length is double the length of the loom, it is possible to allow more warp for the knotting and finishing.

Turn the loom over so that the warp-end bars are facing you. Remove the sword and tension sticks if they are still in the weaving. If you used only one warp-end bar, cut the warp threads at the very edges of both the top and the bottom of the dowel. If you used two dowels, unscrew them, remove the bolts, and cut the warp threads off the dowels. Pull the warp threads out of the heddles. The string heddles can be cut off, retied, and used again if they are long enough.

5-4. Overhand knot.

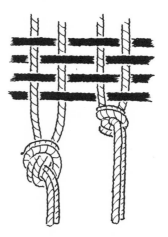

5-5. Warp threads tied in an overhand knot.

EDGING

Edge finishes may be functional—to prevent the fabric from raveling—such as knotted fringes and overhand knots, and they may also be decorative. The nail frame loom usually allows for such a minimum of warp that extra threads must be added for a decorative fringe. You must decide what is best for each project. Some pieces are best left with a clean, simple line or a hard edge rather than an additional border or fringe. Imagine a painting with a fringe, beads, or feathers at the bottom! A decorative addition should never look added or purely decorative—it should be an integral part of the piece. Repeating yarns, colors, textures, techniques, or objects, such as beads, shells, or rocks, that were used in the weaving is usually the best choice (figure 5-6).

5-6. Pamela Hoadly. Hanging. (Courtesy of Gwynne Lott)

Simple Edges

If your project is in a tapestry or weft-faced technique, it can be finished by crisscrossing consecutive pairs of warp threads and pulling them back into the weaving through the opposite adjoining ribs for at least a good inch. Clip the warp threads or knot them. The weft will slip off the warp and unravel if the warp ends are not secured.

Sometimes the weaving comes very close to the edge of the stretchers. In this case the warp should be lifted off the nails rather than cut. Using a threaded tapestry needle, pass through each warp loop and lift it off the nail. You can machine-stitch the edge to secure the threads as long as you roll the edge back and hand-stitch it later (figure 5-7). All handcrafted pieces should be finished by hand.

You can secure the warp edge with twining or with hand stitches such as running stitch, blanket stitch, overcasting, cross-stitching, and hemstitching. Any of these edgestitches can be done before the piece is removed from the frame, while it is still under tension. It is usually necessary to use one of them if the warp ends are too short and too clumsy to knot. Hemstitching (figure 5-8) is excellent for this purpose. Thread your needle with a yarn that blends with or matches the edges. Moving from the right, the needle passes through the fabric 2 warp threads in from the selvage, around the outermost 2 threads, behind the weaving, and up through the fabric at a point 2 warp threads in from the selvage and 2 weft threads in from the edge. Continue the stitch until all the threads at the edge are firmly secured.

If you have taken your piece off the frame loom, the edge may be rolled back and finished with a hem. The hem should be sewn with small, inconspicuous, invisible stitches and fine sewing thread. The size of the hem varies with the project and with the amount of extra material available. Make sure to allow for the hem when you weave the heading into the project, or parts of the design may be covered up by the hem. It is better to have a few extra rows that can be raveled out than such a short heading and edge that the piece cannot be finished. A protective heading may be woven in before the regular heading, which you can use for the finish and ravel out later.

A project that will be seen on only one side may be finished with seam binding on the reverse side. Sew the binding tape along the edge by hand or with a sewing machine, trim, turn back, and hem down by hand. If your piece is intended to hang, you can slip weights or a rod into the hem. Or you can sew circular hoops or hooks on the back.

Another possibility is to line the entire piece and back it with another piece of fabric after it has been blocked and shaped. You can sew a pocket in the top of the lining, as with a curtain, to provide a slit for the hanging rod. In backing a project be sure that both the weaving and the lining are squared at right angles. Pin them together before sewing them with small stitches at least 1/2" apart.

5-7. Rolled hem. (Photo: Hector Garcia)

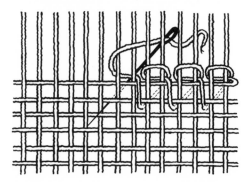

5-8. Hemstitching.

Decorative Edges

The warp ends are usually very short on a frame loom, leaving little if any excess for decorative edges, finishes, or fringes. If you plan ahead, however, it is possible to add extra threads that can be treated in any number of ways.

A precut-pile technique such as rya is ideal for adding a fringe as a decorative border, since the strands may combine different lengths, colors, or textures. The strands may be macraméd, braided, knotted, shaped, cut, or finished in practically any technique that is suitable to the project.

After you have woven the heading, add a row or more of the precut pile with a rya knot. The decorative edge can be as long as you like, even two or three times as long as the weaving. The edge should function not as an additional border but as part of the whole piece (figure 5-9). Roll the heading back and hem, then remove the piece from the loom. The fringe will hang down and cover the edge. Edges shaped into curved or triangular shapes are exciting forms to try (figure 5-10).

5-9. Bonnie Kondor. Wall hanging. (Photo: Hector Garcia)

5-10. Odette Brabec. Hanging. The edge of a hanging may be woven into a shape. The unwoven warp threads are either pulled inside the ribs, cut, and woven into the weaving as a weft or knotted and used as a decorative fringe. (Photo: Hector Garcia)

A snitch knot, also known as a reversed-double-half-hitch macramé knot, is another way to add fringe after the weaving has been removed from the loom. Cut strands are added to a piece that has already been hemmed. Each strand should be twice the length of the final fringe, since it will be doubled over. Many combinations of weights, colors, textures, and lengths can easily be incorporated.

To make a snitch knot, thread a tapestry needle with a strand of yarn and insert it into the right side of the fabric, through to the wrong side, and back up to the right side, leaving a loop on the wrong side (figure 5-11). Pull the ends of the strand evenly through this loop and tighten to produce a snitch knot. The width and the spacing of the knot depend on the desired density and the thickness of the yarn.

A snitch knot may be used to add beads or other objects with a core or hole to the weaving. Double the strand over, pass it through a hole in the object, and pull tight. The ends may be woven or used as a fringe. Objects can also be slipped on the cut fringe and secured with knotting, braiding, or wrapping. Feathers can be added by tying the quills in with wrapped yarn.

A hanging device, a rod, or an object such as a stem or a branch can be inserted and held in place by a continuous weft of a loop technique such as Ghiordes knots or pulled loops. Weave the weft in plain weave for part of the row and use it as a knot and a loop to secure the object in other areas (figure 5-12). The tension of the loops is easy to adapt to varying thicknesses or curves. If the object is shaped, the edge of the weaving may be altered to follow the contour. After you have secured the object, add a plain-weave heading for the finish and the hem.

Anything may be used for a hanging rod. Wooden doweling wrapped with yarn is an attractive choice. Cover the rod with a light coat of colorless glue and wind the yarn evenly around the rod. Or try a branch, a metal rod, a piece of wood—anything that fits in with the character of the piece (figure 5-13).

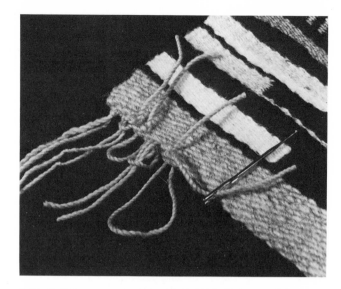

5-11. Snitch, or reversed-double-half-hitch macramé, knot. (Photo: Hector Garcia)

5-12. Finished piece, with rya fringe at the bottom and a hanging rod held in place with Ghiordes-knot loops. The edges are all that remain to be finished. (Photo: Hector Garcia)

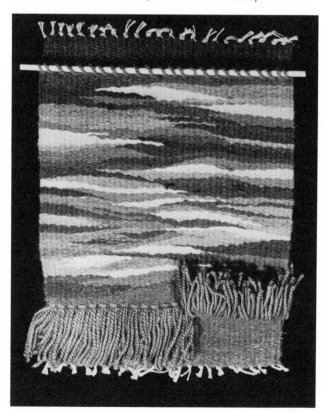

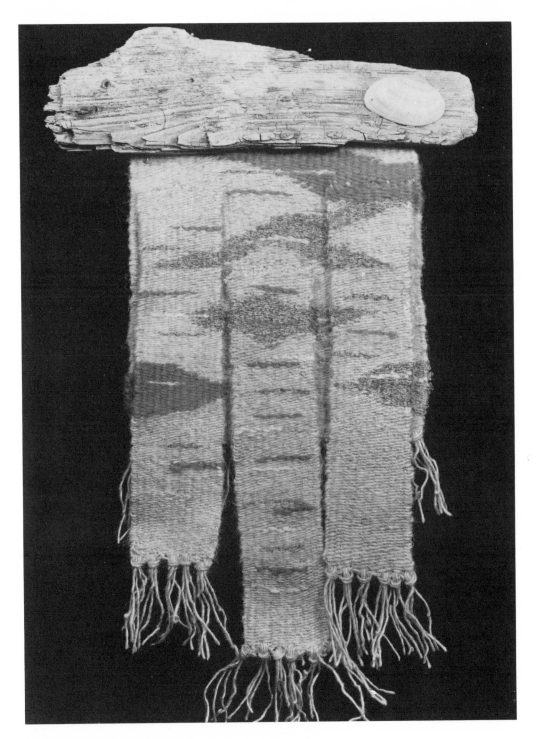

5-13. Birgit Shand. Hanging, woven in four separate pieces, sewn together, and tacked down to wood. (Photo: Hector Garcia)

Several woven pieces can be joined together to create another design such as a rug or a wall hanging (figure 5-14). To join slits or separate pieces together, use a fine, strong thread. Encircle each warp thread on both sides between each line of weft (figure 5-15). The joining should be smooth, and the stitches should not show on the right side. A curved upholstery needle is helpful.

5-14. Stephanie Whiting. Tapestry strips sewn together to create another form. (Photo: Robert Fields)

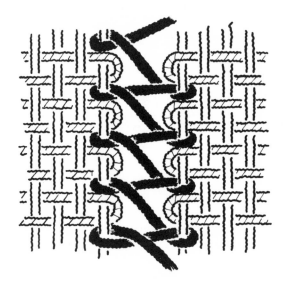

5-15. Joining two slits or woven pieces together.

BLOCKING

Tapestries, wall hangings, and many small projects need to be blocked in order to be shaped and squared. There are two methods that you can use: (1) Tack the fabric down to a flat surface at short intervals, moisten it with water, and dry slowly, away from sunlight and excessive heat. (2) Pin the weaving to a padded surface, place a damp cloth over it, and steam-iron. Do not press down. If the weaving does not need a great deal of blocking, the steam iron may be used with a dry cloth. Just press—do not use a circular or scrubbing movement, which might distort the weaving.

CLEANING

Depending on the yarns used, most projects can either be washed or dry-cleaned. It is advisable to clean most projects, particularly large, functional ones, after they are finished to remove soil that has accumulated during weaving and to bind the yarns closer together. Pile and shag pieces may be shaken free of accumulated dust.

A good craftsman always ensures the durability of his work. This begins with a selection of good-quality materials suitable to the project and does not end until the piece is properly finished. With some projects such as wall hangings or sculpture the work is not complete until the piece is installed and shown to the best advantage. Concern with minor details is the mark of the person who loves what he creates.

CHAPTER 6.

DESIGN

To design is to create order and to establish meaning by planning and arranging separate elements and parts into a comprehensive whole that conveys the intentions of the designer. The craft and process of weaving give the fabric form and structure by combining threads and techniques to produce a surface that has texture, color, and shape. The materials and constructions give the fabric physical form. Through design form gains purpose, expression, and significance. Form is therefore a combination of both physical structure and visual characteristics.

It is not possible to fully understand why a particular design is successful. After all the parts have been explained, there is still the mystery of the viewer's participation in the piece. It is an experience that reaches out and is felt emotionally as well as intellectually.

Design implies order, but order is not stifling. When an order or arrangement is a planned sequence, a deliberate action or decision intended to produce a specific effect, even a series of loops, knots, tangles, and fringes may be worked out as part of a design and considered to be in order. The question is whether the particular selection and arrangement best expresses the idea, fulfills its purpose, and does what it is intended to do.

Every person who makes something is designing, whether the process is conscious or subconscious. Design involves selecting colors, textures, techniques, and shapes. As soon as a particular yarn is selected rather than another, the weaver is designing. Whether it is controlled or spontaneous, the selection contains certain inherent visual qualities, and the weaver is sensitive in some way to the relationships between them.

In planning a design there are three major factors to consider: (1) what is the thought, the content, the idea, the goal, and the purpose of the piece; (2) how can it be expressed through design—what shapes, colors, and textures reinforce the idea and how may they be organized to convey the feeling and the concept and to fulfill the intentions of the designer; (3) which techniques and materials are best suited to the project? The last factor is important because it is the channel through which an image in the mind becomes a physical reality and a presence.

CONTENT

Every person has something unique and special to say. We all have visual experiences and insights into our environment and surroundings. The manner in which we communicate and translate ideas is as varied as the individuals themselves. Every experience is valid as a resource for expression.

The weaver responds to an inner personal need to create forms with fibers. The inspiration may come from the color and texture of the yarns; the sensuous quality of the fibers; the challenge of a particular technique; or a personal vision, idea, or design that may best be expressed in fibers and yarns.

The creative weaver combines imagination and intuition with an understanding of the principles of design and a mastery of exacting skills and disciplines to create an aesthetic entity (figure 6-1). Ideas may develop from materials and techniques, associations, natural objects, human nature, our own personalities, visions, dreams—anything that the weaver finds enjoyable and exciting enough to become involved with to the point of feeling compelled to create.

6-1. *Front d/Arago*. Joseph Grau-Garriga. Wool and cotton, 1973, 88″ × 117″. (Collection of Arris Gallery, New York; courtesy of Los Angeles County Museum of Art)

DESIGN

A design may be objective or figurative; it may have literary associations; it may be an abstraction composed of colors, textures, and forms that are meaningful within themselves as a satisfying arrangement of visual elements. Weaving today shares a common vocabulary with painting and sculpture.

Whatever the source or the basis for a design, the weaver who is a designer and possibly an artist follows a direction with his whole personality. The act of creation demands self-awareness and honesty. The designer-weaver must rely on inner resources and develop the ability to determine the best means of conveying his thought.

TECHNIQUE

The vehicle for expression and creativity is technique, or craft. Craft represents the skills, disciplines, and technical competence that are necessary to follow through and give physical structure and effectiveness to an idea. Technique is not an obstacle or a stopping point but a framework that challenges the weaver to explore and go beyond the merely technical aspects. As a designer the weaver is constantly exploring the visual world, the world of inner feelings and images, and the characteristics of his materials. The craft is the foundation that the weaver works from and struggles with to give birth to something new. Beautiful technique is stale without imagination, just as the best design will not be effective if the weaver does not have the skill to give it a durable physical structure. There must be a balance between the two.

Inspiration requires materials and techniques to interpret experience. The hands manipulating the threads must work with the mind. The mind must have a channel, the craft through which thought can establish meaning in a tangible form. The structure, the manner in which a woven surface is constructed, is inseparable from its visual characteristics and arrangement. They interact and exert an influence on each other. Some yarn, thread, fiber material, and technique must be used to form a shape. The material and the technique that create the shape are also forming the surface. It is impossible to discuss the visual elements of a woven design without considering the characteristics of the construction. The creative weaver understands both the technical aspects that give physical structure to a woven piece and the elements that give visual structure and meaning to what is seen.

VISUAL ELEMENTS

When a design is complete, everything is interacting in a harmonious accord. Nothing seems out of place. Whether a design is very active and complex or very simple, all the elements reinforce the concept. Everything shares the visual characteristics of line, shape, color, and texture. All things that are visible occupy some type of space. The combinations of visual elements are infinite: they cannot be separated from each other except as an abstraction. It is an excellent habit, however, to try to distinguish the characteristics that make one object different from or similar to another. You will develop an awareness of how objects are perceived.

Line

Line is the basic element of weaving. The very nature of the weaving process is to form a whole from small parts, and the lines—the threads in the warp and weft—are the smallest units. Yarns as lines possess inherent qualities of softness, hardness, color, sheen, and texture; they seem to possess personality, a suggestive quality of energy and vitality (figure 6-2). A line in a linen is not the same as in a mohair, looped, slubbed, or novelty yarn. The weight, twist, and combination of fibers change the appearance of the line, or thread. The same design may be executed in different materials and different weaves, and each time the appearance and function of the design will change.

Lines create patterns of movement and rhythms (figure 6-3). They suggest direction and motion in a variety of ways: they can be straight, curved, zigzag, or jagged; they can be seen in isolation or with other lines. Lines are part of the weaving construction, formed by the interlocking of threads, and they are seen as part of the design.

Lines can be broad or narrow. As a visual element lines of varying width give the impression of shading or distance: changes in space are indicated by changing the sizes of the lines (figure 6-4). Tension is created when lines of varying widths are compressed and concentrated, then expanded and spaced widely apart.

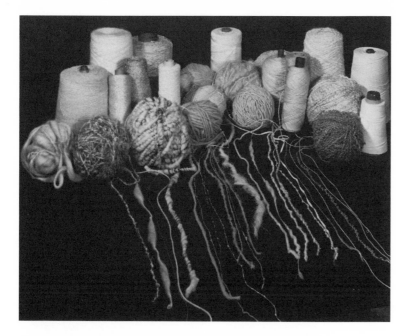

6-2. The physical structure of a fabric is composed of the vertical and horizontal lines in the warp and weft, i.e., the threads and yarns. (Photo: Hector Garcia)

6-3. *Sign 1970–71.* Benedikte and Jan Groth. Tapestry weave, cotton warp, wool weft, Danish, 1970–71, 111″ × 180″. (Courtesy of the Collection Provinciehuis Noord-Brabant, 's-Hertogenbosch, the Netherlands)

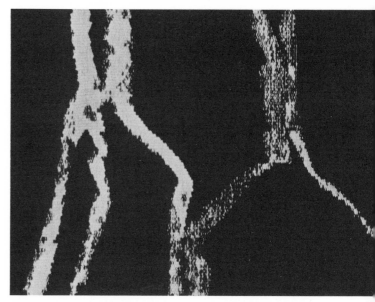

6-4. *Sign 1971–72* (detail). Benedikte and Jan Groth. Tapestry weave, cotton warp, wool weft, Danish, 1971–72, 86 1/2″ × 125″. (Courtesy of Jan Groth)

123

Horizontal lines and shapes with a horizontal axis are peaceful, balanced, serene. They pull the eye of the viewer across the piece from side to side. Since weaving evolves row by row and line by line, the weft tends to produce dominant horizontal movements.

Vertical lines give a feeling of height. If horizontal lines pull the eye across a surface from side to side, vertical lines pull the eye up and down. The weaver has to make a conscious effort to concentrate on vertical lines and shapes and to break away from the strong horizontal tendency. This is possible in tapestry and pictorial weaving, since the weaver has direct control over the design and can work out some sections before others. The whole piece need not develop simultaneously in a line from side to side. Egyptian and Swedish knots and wrapping techniques produce a strong vertical construction. Rya knots can be seen as vertical lines, but they appear to pull downward, especially if they are close to the bottom of a piece.

Diagonal lines and shapes suggest agitation. They are not balanced but seem to tip in one direction or the other. They are like pointing arrows. The techniques that hang, curl, twist, wrap, loop, and intertwine have a direction and suggest movement (figure 6-5).

Different yarns and techniques give different qualities to the lines. A line may be seen as an edge, a contour of a plane, a surface (figure 6-6). If a line closes in on itself, it becomes a shape: a knot, for example, is a shape formed by a single line. Several knots form a larger shape that has an outline (figure 6-7).

Threads are often used to construct shapes that move in the opposite direction to the technique. Soumak and twill, for example, move on a diagonal but can be contained within a square, which is a vertical-horizontal shape. Plain weave is composed of vertical and horizontal lines. It is a perfectly balanced construction, yet visual illusions contrary to the structure may be created, such as the diagonal lines produced in tapestry weaving.

It is important to realize that all of the larger areas and shapes that form a piece are composed and constructed from lines, and these lines lend their personality to the character of the whole.

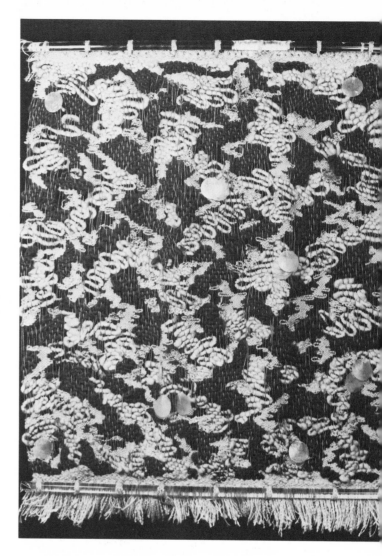

6-5. Noreen Rubin. Hanging. (Photo: Hector Garcia)

6-6. Winifred Bondareff. Design based on a Mexican postage stamp. (Photo: Robert Fields)

6-7. Lucille Frasca. Sampler of techniques woven as a landscape. Each knot functions as a separate simple shape and builds into a larger shape. The repetition of the knots creates a texture that interacts with the texture of the yarn. (Courtesy of the artist)

Shape

Shapes can be geometric or free-form; both are found in nature. Geometric shapes—rectangles, squares, and triangles—are used quite frequently by weavers, since they are compatible with the horizontal-vertical interlacement of the warp and weft (figure 6-8). Ovals and circles are built in a series of tiny steps or by manipulating and shaping the threads. Nongeometric free-form shapes lack a tight, rigid edge. They are usually composed of curving or irregular contour lines but retain a proportionate rhythmic repeat (figure 6-9). Hatching, hachures, rounded lozenges, and ovals work well for free-form shapes. They are easier to develop horizontally on the weft than vertically on the warp, which is why many free-form pieces are woven horizontally, then turned at a 90° angle and hung vertically (figure 6-10).

Small shapes can be repeated to build larger shapes just as lines can be repeated to build shapes. In weaving it is the repetition and grouping of the same yarns in the same techniques that give a shape its predominant character. A shape may be combined with other different shapes—shapes designed to be seen in relationship to each other—but each individual shape is composed of similar characteristics (figure 6-11).

6-8. *Seashore*. Nancy Sullivan. (Photo: Hector Garcia)

6-9. Sheri La Plante. Shaped sculptural piece. (Courtesy of the artist)

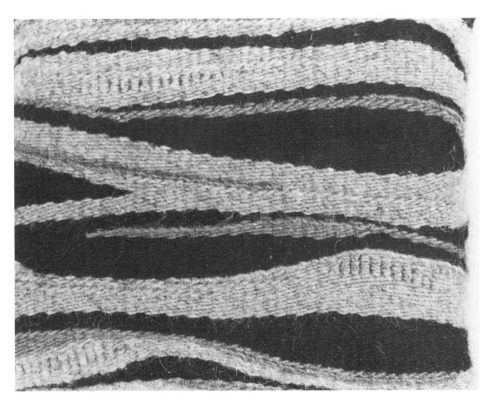

6-10. Stephanie Whiting. Pillow. (Photo: Robert Fields)

6-11. Sheri La Plante. Sculptural form. The same organic shape is repeated three times. (Courtesy of the artist)

Space

Everything that is seen is perceived as occupying space. Space indicates the area between shapes and the distance or depth from one shape to the next. The space may be the actual physical space occupied by a piece (figure 6-14) or an illusion of space created by visual clues on a two-dimensional flat surface (figure 6-15).

The space surrounding a shape is defined by that shape. Space and shape are interdependent and perceived through each other. If you hold your hand up close to your face with your fingers spread out, the fingers function as shapes. The area between each finger is perceived as space. If you change the position of your hand and bend your fingers, the intervening spaces change and are reorganized into different shapes and patterns. The fingers and the spaces are related to each other.

A background that is not occupied by a shape or figure is called *negative space. Positive space* refers to a space that is occupied by figures or forms. The terms "positive" (shape) and "negative" (space) are sometimes misleading, since a negative space also has shape; it is just as important as a figure in the visual structure. What is seen as an object can often be seen as the area or space that surrounds another object. The roles of figure and ground are dual and interchangeable. You have only to look around any room or outdoors in the city or country to realize how complicated—or how simple—the relationship between shape and space can become.

If some areas in a woven piece are left open, they change the original shape, and the areas that are seen through are integrated into the weaving (figure 6-16).

The weaver simultaneously creates a surface and the spaces and shapes that occupy that surface. Weaving is different from painting, drawing, or needlework, in which the canvas, paper, or fabric background already exists. The weaver must be aware that everything has shape, color, and texture and that one shape depends on the shape that preceded it and exists beside it. The manner in which the spaces and shapes are organized gives form and structure to a piece.

The experience of seeing is a spatial experience: a sense of space is developed. Children explore space until they acquire an understanding of how they see and are able to recognize objects in familiar and unfamiliar situations. Space may be expressed as an illusion, as a representation of what is seen, as a concept that is understood, or as a representation of space as it is thought to be. It is interesting that the expression and application of space in art have evolved along with changes in the scientific concept of space. We have moved from a flat world arranged in bands through the world of perspective into a world that includes temporal duration. What is seen and how it is seen depends on the vocabulary and awareness, the terms and concepts that the viewer brings to his perception.

6-14. Sheri La Plante. Sculpture. (Courtesy of the artist)

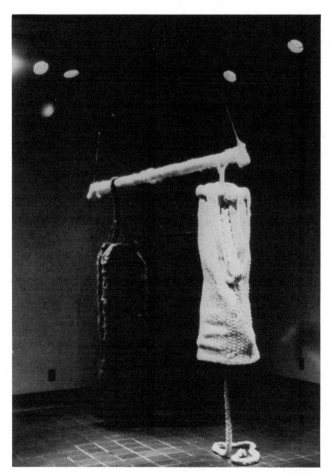

6-15. *Procession of the Fat Ox.* Daniel Leyniers the Younger. From a cartoon by David Teniers, tapestry weave, wool and silk, Flemish, early 18th century, 144″ × 130″. (Courtesy of the Art Institute of Chicago)

There are two kinds of space to keep in mind in relation to weaving: (1) the actual physical space that a piece occupies and (2) the space that is indicated within the piece. The viewer must have visual cues to interpret his relationship to the object. A piece that is larger than the viewer makes him feel smaller. He has to move his head and body in order to understand what is happening. If a weaving is three-dimensional, it has to be handled or moved around to understand all its sides. Fabrics whose original shape has been changed have to be moved to perceive the relationship between the parts. A large piece displayed in a small area can be so overwhelming that it is unbearable. Likewise, a small piece in a large area can become insignificant. A small weaving can hold the attention of the viewer and become compelling through its color and pattern. A large weaving can become bland and uninteresting. Largeness for its own sake is a mistake: the concept, function, and design of a piece should be compatible with the size. As an idea evolves through experimentation, a sense of the proper size will also evolve naturally. The opposite is also true: given a predetermined space, the weaver will begin to visualize which sizes and shapes seem most comfortable inside it.

A small weaving is comprehended at once. It occupies a small area and can be held; the viewer—and the weaver—are larger and in control. Sometimes the very smallness of an object inspires a feeling of protectiveness. The small frame loom is not at all intimidating and leaves the weaver free to experiment easily. As his confidence grows and ideas take shape, he can move on to a larger frame loom or transfer his ideas to another loom that allows for bigger dimensions.

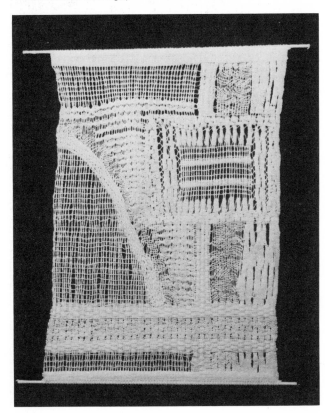

6-16. *Lace Hanging.* Julia Lettell. Hanging, woven in leno, Danish medallions, and Spanish lace in regular and irregular groups. A metal rod wrapped with yarn adds weight to the bottom of the piece and increases the tension on the warp threads. The open spaces are part of the design and are integrated into the weaving as part of the visual whole. Space and form are both parts of the visual structure. (Photo: Hector Garcia)

131

Most people think of space in art in terms of perspective, which pulls the viewer into the painting and vanishes in the distance. The following suggestions are ways of creating a sensation of space and depth on a flat surface that are equally valid and effective. They may overlap and reinforce other spatial cues that have already been established.

The size and proportions of a woven piece are referred to as the *format.* A shape placed on the format is called a *figure*, and the area around it the *ground* (figure 6-17). Scale is important: a figure surrounded by a large area of ground appears smaller than the same figure compressed into a smaller format. A group of small shapes surrounded by ground can easily become weak if there is no attraction or tension between them. If the shapes almost touch, there is visual tension; the further away they are from each other, the less tension there is. The viewer also tends to group similar colors, shapes, and textures together, reading them as a single pattern.

If parts of the figure touch the edges of the format and the shape of the ground is as interesting as the figure, it becomes difficult to determine which is the figure and which is the ground. The relationship is ambiguous, and the viewer bounces back and forth between the two. Combinations of black and white or of strong contrasting colors are effective in this arrangement (figure 6-18). Many optical illusions and flat pattern repeats are based on a shifting figure-ground relationship. Quilt patterns are an excellent source of examples.

Objects, shapes, and figures that are close to the viewer are sharper and clearer in detail. They are brighter and larger. Large shapes will appear to move forward no matter where they are placed. The more active a pattern is, the closer it seems. A pattern with a rough texture will also appear closer. Yarns and knots can be used to create a feeling of space. Heavy threads and areas that are heavy in texture will advance. Smoother, thin, less textured threads will recede. Smaller, grayer shapes will seem to be a long way off in the distance.

If one object overlaps and covers part of another, the viewer assumes from experience that the first is in front of the second. Spatial patterns can be produced by overlapping different sizes or shapes. If the shapes are opaque, figure-ground relationships appear fixed; if color is used to give the illusion of transparency, new relationships are created. A shape may appear to be first in front of and then behind another shape. If many shapes are transparent or mixed with opaque shapes or changes in size, the whole piece seems to move back and forth. This shifting is a subjective, metaphysical sensation of depth.

Many artists have expressed distance as a series of flat, horizontal bands stacked on top of one another. The higher the figure, the further back it is supposed to be. Repetition of shapes overlapping each other was also used to indicate space.

Converging diagonal lines and shapes pull the viewer into the space. They appear to expand or contract, to come out of or go into the space, depending on the point at which they come together.

Advancing and receding colors and value changes create a sensation of space. White seems to advance; black seems to recede. If white shapes are used with other colors, they often appear to be spotty, floating, and unrelated. Strong light and dark colors are difficult to control if they are used with other colors. Very dark colors sometimes appear to recede and produce visual holes.

This simplified discussion of space is intended to serve as a starting point in exploring and understanding how an image is structured. Space acts as a container of shapes, but there can be many different kinds of containers. Everything—every figure, object, and shape—is located in space. The space may appear as a simple ground, a surface with a flat figure on it; the ground may be perceived as a space bending around a volume defined by planes, or the figures may overlap and be arranged in more complicated relationships. The sensation and perception of space come through looking at things and questioning how they are seen.

6-17. *Streaker*. Julia Lettell. (Photo: Hector Garcia)

6-18. *Gris*, *noir*, *rouge*. Designed by Jean Arp, woven at the Atelier Tabard Frères et Soeurs. Tapestry weave, wool, 1958, 60 3/8″ × 52 3/8″. (Courtesy of the Art Institute of Chicago)

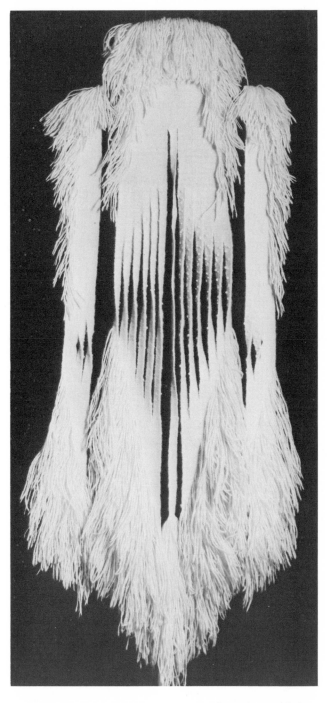

6-19. Marilyn Ruck. Tapestry woven on a frame loom side by side in three separate pieces. The tapestry strips were twisted into a subtle spiral. (Photo: Hector Garcia)

133

STRUCTURAL ELEMENTS

Besides the visual elements of line, shape, color, texture, and space there are other structural principles of design—rhythm, proportion, emphasis, and balance.

Rhythm

The repetition of elements creates a rhythm and establishes a pattern. Rhythm in design is the same concept as rhythm in music—it is used to distinguish one composition from another.

The recurrence of patterns, spaces, lines, textures, colors, and shapes produces a visual movement that directs the viewer's perception of the design. The viewer tends to group similar elements together and to see the separate parts as a unit. The rhythm varies in each piece, depending on how it is organized. A checkerboard composed of identical shapes produces an even, static rhythm. The rhythm is marked by the expected occurrence or recurrence of an element.

Proportion

Proportion, scale, or ratio is a comparison of the size, quantity, and mass of—or the relationship between—the elements in the design. The elements are relative to each other. Proportion refers to the changes in size of the elements as well as to the scale of the woven article as compared to the space in which it is seen.

Emphasis

The purpose of emphasis is to attract attention to the main theme of the design or to a specific focal point. Planning eliminates details that clutter and distract the viewer. Emphasizing does not mean eliminating all details—only those that are not pertinent to the design.

Balance

When two objects of the same size and shape are placed at an equal distance from the center of a design, they are in equal, or formal, balance. This is called a *symmetrical* pattern and is produced by identical mirror images on all sides. If a smaller object is placed further from the center than a larger object, balance is unequal, or *asymmetrical.* An asymmetrical design may still be balanced. A smaller object that is vivid in color may seem to balance a larger object that is weak in color. Color, shape, and texture can all be adjusted to achieve a balanced composition. The subjective feeling of equilibrium depends on the distribution of visual weight. Visual weight involves all of the elements and principles of weaving—the placement of shapes, the yarns, and the techniques.

THE CREATIVE PROCESS

Before you begin to design, it is most important to understand the advantages, potentials, and restrictions of weaving as a craft. The designer who is in control has the discipline needed to make the image and the craft compatible with each other. In other words, control implies selecting the yarns, constructions, and forms that best convey the idea. A piece may appear very free, organic, and spontaneous and yet involve just as much planning and control as a very tight, flat, formal design. Each approach requires the discipline necessary to achieve the intended impression and result.

It is difficult to design on paper or in another medium and then try to translate the drawing into a weaving. Before working out your ideas on paper, it is useful to first weave many small samples and experiment to see which fibers, constructions, shapes, and textures produce the desired effects. You will also discover which kinds of forms and images are possible. Experimenting develops the imagination and suggests new possibilities. No large project should be undertaken without first investigating the design in smaller-scale samples and studies.

Work in a relaxed atmosphere in which your mind is open to suggestion rather than with a preconceived idea in a restricted, uncomfortable atmosphere. An idea cannot be forced. You may struggle to evolve a concept, but you have to pass through a series of experiences before you can understand the best combinations for the project. No one has enough imagination to anticipate at the beginning what the finished piece will look like. As the design evolves, the medium and the interaction of the materials give it character and life.

Designing and creating images is a process in

which you must be open to what the project itself suggests as it grows. Proportion, the placement of shapes, and the general arrangement of elements may be planned in advance, but they must also be subject to change if something unexpected and exciting begins to happen. Creating woven images is a visual experience and a dialogue with the materials. We start as children with a small vocabulary, but as we become more aware of what we see and how we feel about what we see, we begin to build a system of visual communication.

The frame loom is a simple tool, but it is not limiting. With imagination it may easily become the starting point for individual expression and creativity. Its simplicity is an advantage that allows for the greatest freedom in developing design potential. The intention of this book is to show that an idea may be developed in a very simple and direct manner. The success of a design is not determined by size, technique, or mechanical sophistication of the loom but rather by the ability of the weaver to use any loom to full advantage in expressing his or her design.

BIBLIOGRAPHY

DESIGN

Albers, Anni. *On Designing.* New Haven: Pelango Press, 1959.

Albers, Josef. *Interaction of Color.* New Haven: Yale University Press, 1963.

Anderson, Donald M. *Elements of Design.* New York: Holt, Rinehart, and Winston, 1961.

Bager, Bertel. *Nature as Designer.* New York: Van Nostrand Reinhold Company, 1966.

Birren, Faber. *Creative Color.* New York: Van Nostrand Reinhold Company, 1972.

Blumenau, Lili. *Creative Design in Wallhangings.* New York: Crown, 1967.

Chevreul, M. E. *Principles of Harmony and Contrasts of Colors.* New York: Van Nostrand Reinhold Company, 1967.

Constantine, Mildred and Larsen, Jack Lenor. *Beyond Craft: The Art Fabric.* Van Nostrand Reinhold Company, 1972.

De Montebello, Philippe. *Grau-Garriga.* Houston: The Museum of Fine Arts, 1971.

De Sausmerez, Maurice. *Basic Design: The Dynamics of Visual Form.* New York: Van Nostrand Reinhold Company, 1973.

Garrett, Lillian. *Visual Design.* New York: Van Nostrand Reinhold Company, 1966.

Guyler, Vivian Vardey. *Design in Nature.* Worcester, Massachusetts: Davis Publications, Inc., 1970.

Hartung, Rolf. *Creative Textile Design: Thread and Fabric.* New York: Van Nostrand Reinhold Company, 1964.

Itten, Johannes. *The Art of Color.* New York: Van Nostrand Reinhold Company, 1966.

Johnson, Meda P. and Kaufman, Glen. *Design on Fabrics.* New York: Van Nostrand Reinhold Company, 1967.

Kepes, Gyorgy. *Vision and Value* Series. New York: George Braziller, 1965.

Proctor, Richard M. *Principles of Pattern.* New York: Van Nostrand Reinhold Company, 1969.

TAPESTRY

Beutlich, Tadek. *The Technique of Woven Tapestry.* New York: Watson-Guptill Publications, 1971.

Coffinet, Julien and Pianzola, Maurice. *Tapestry.* New York: Van Nostrand Reinhold Company, 1972.

Forman, B. and W. and Wassef, Ramses Wissa. *Tapestries from Egypt Woven by the Children of Harrania.* London: Hamlyn, 1961.

Jobe, Joseph, ed. *Great Tapestries: The Web of History from the 12th to the 20th Century.* Translated by Peggy Rovell and Edith Lausanne Obserson. New York: Time-Life Books, 1965.

Kahlenberg, Mary Hunt and Berlant, Anthony. *The Navajo Blanket.* New York: A. Praeger, Inc., 1968.

Kaufmann, Ruth. *New American Tapestry.* New York: Reinhold, 1968.

Sevensma, W. S. *Tapestries.* New York: Universe Books, 1965.

OTHER CONSTRUCTIONS AND METHODS

Collingwood, Peter. *The Techniques of Rug Weaving.* New York: Watson-Guptill Publications, 1968.

D'Harcourt, Raoul. *Textiles of Ancient Peru and Their Techniques.* Seattle: University of Washington Press, 1962.

Harvey, Virginia I. *Macramé: The Art of Creative Knotting.* New York: Van Nostrand Reinhold Company, 1967.

Meilach, Dona Z. *Macramé: Creative Design in Knotting.* New York: Crown Publishers, Inc., 1971.

Tattersall, C. E. C. *Notes on Carpet Knotting and Weaving.* London: Victoria and Albert Museum, 1961.

Willcox, Donald. *The Technique of Rya Knotting.* New York: Van Nostrand Reinhold Company, 1971.

Wilson, Jean. *The Pile Weaves.* New York: Van Nostrand Reinhold Company, 1974.

———. *Weaving is For Anyone.* New York: Van Nostrand Reinhold Company, 1966.

————. *Weaving is Creative.* New York: Van Nostrand Reinhold Company, 1972.

————. *Weaving is Fun.* New York: Van Nostrand Reinhold Company, 1971.

————. *Weaving You Can Use.* New York: Van Nostrand Reinhold Company, 1975.

————. *Weaving You Can Wear.* New York: Van Nostrand Reinhold Company, 1973.

Znamierowski, Nell. *Step-by-Step Rugmaking.* New York: Golden Press, Inc., 1972.

GENERAL READING

Albers, Anni. *On Weaving.* Middletown, Conn.: Wesleyan University Press, 1965.

Birrell Verla. *The Textile Arts.* New York: Harper and Brothers, 1959.

Emery, Irene. *Primary Structures of Fabrics.* Washington, D. C.: Textile Museum, 1966.

Held, Shirley E. *Weaving: A Handbook for Fiber Craftsmen.* New York: Holt, Rinehart, and Winston, 1973.

Mayer, Christa C. *Masterpieces of Western Textiles from the Art Institute of Chicago.* Chicago: 1969.

Regensteiner, Else. *The Art of Weaving.* New York: Van Nostrand Reinhold Company, 1970.

————. *Weaver's Study Course: Ideas and Techniques.* New York: Van Nostrand Reinhold Company, 1975.

Zielinski, S. A. *Encyclopedia of Hand Weaving.* New York: Funk and Wagnalls, 1959.

PERIODICALS

Craft Horizons
American Craftsmen's Council
44 West 53rd Street
New York, New York 10019

Handweaver and Craftsman
220 Fifth Avenue
New York, New York 10001

Shuttle, Spindle, and Dye-pot
998 Farmington Avenue
West Hartford, Connecticut 06107

The Working Craftsman
Box 42
Northbrook, Illinois 60062

VISUAL GLOSSARY OF TECHNIQUES

TAPESTRY

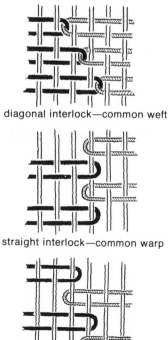

plain weave

straight interlock—common weft

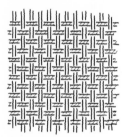

straight slit

diagonal interlock—common weft

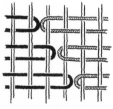

diagonal slit

straight interlock—common warp

diagonal interlock—common warp

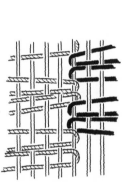

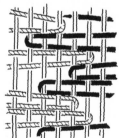

dovetailing—regular groups

dovetailing—irregular groups

lozenges

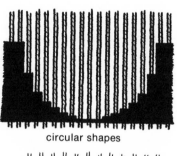

circular shapes

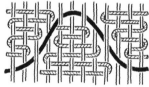

outling with plain weave

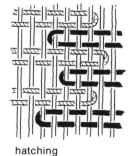

hatching

PILE WEAVES

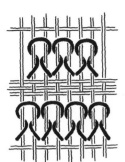

Ghiordes knot (cut)

Greek soumak

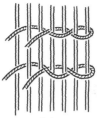

twining

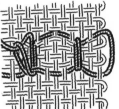

bouquets

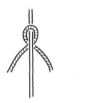

Ghiordes knot (uncut)

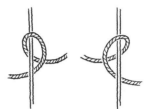

single soumak

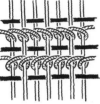

Egyptian knot

Danish medallion

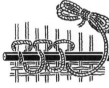

Senna knot

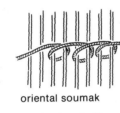

oriental soumak

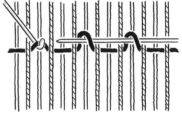

pulled loops

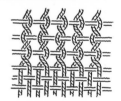

leno (gauze weave)

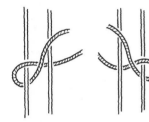

Spanish knot

Swedish knot

Spanish lace—regular groups

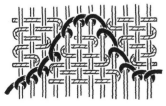

outlining with soumak

chaining

Spanish lace—irregular groups

139

GLOSSARY

balanced weave—a weave in which the number of warp threads per inch is equal to the number of weft threads per inch.

basic weave—a system of thread interlacement, or weaving construction, that is not derived from any other system. The basic weaves are **plain weave, twill,** and **satin.**

basket weave—a derivative of plain weave created by interlacing 2 or more warp threads with 2 or more weft threads.

basse lisse—a tapestry woven on a horizontal handloom; low-warp tapestry.

bouclé yarn—a looped novelty yarn.

bouquet—a method of creating lace in which a weft thread is wrapped around several warp threads to draw them together.

brocade—a decorative yarn added to a plain ground such as plain weave.

cable yarn—a yarn composed of two or more yarn plies twisted together.

cartoon—a design used as a guide in weaving a tapestry.

chroma—see intensity.

color pattern—pattern formed by a combination of weaves and colors.

Danish medallion—a method of producing lace in which the weft departs from the usual horizontal position to form a loop on the surface of the web.

design—a plan that establishes order and meaning through the arrangement of separate elements into a comprehensive whole that conveys the intentions of the designer.

discontinuous weave—any weave in which the weft threads do not pass from selvage to selvage but appear in specific areas of the web.

double weave—a weave that produces two distinct layers, usually connected at some point.

eccentric weft—a weft thread that departs from the usual horizontal position to move in arcs at acute angles to the warp; used in tapestry.

end—an individual warp thread.

fiber—the material, natural or synthetic, from which yarn is spun.

filament fiber—a fiber that is measured in yards; reeled silk and all man-made fibers are filament lengths.

filling—see weft.

finger weave—a weave produced by manipulating individual warp threads with the fingers or a pickup stick.

frame loom—any simple square, rectangular, or circular loom, usually without harnesses or a beater.

gauze—an open weave produced by twisting warp threads around each other; also called **leno.**

haute lisse—a tapestry woven on an upright vertical loom; high-warp tapestry.

heading—the beginning and ending bands of a fabric.

hue—the pure state of any color; the family to which a color belongs, such as red, yellow, orange, blue, green, or violet.

inlay—see laid-in weave.

intensity—the relative purity or grayness of a color.

lace weave—an openwork characterized by a distortion of the warp or weft threads from the parallel position.

laid-in weave—a weaver-controlled weave in which decorative pattern threads are added to a plain-weave ground in selected areas of the web.

leno—a lace weave produced by crossing selected warp threads in a pattern before inserting the weft.

loom—any device that holds the warp threads taut and in their proper positions.

loom-controlled weave—any weave that is produced through the interaction of the heddles and harnesses on a loom.

macramé—a technique of knotting threads.

novelty yarn—a complex yarn that has irregularities in size and twist.

pattern weave—a design formed by threading and treadling arrangements, based on the repetition of the same unit.

pick—a line of weft put through the warp; also called a **shot.**

pick count—the number of weft threads per inch, as compared to the sett of the warp.

pickup stick—a flat, pointed stick used for making hand-controlled patterns.

pile—yarns that create a surface that is raised above a flat background.

plain weave—a simple over-and-under pattern of alternate interlocking warp and weft threads.

ply yarn—a yarn in which 2 or more single strands are twisted together.

primary color—a color that cannot be mixed from other colors; red, yellow, and blue.

roving—an untwisted yarn; a condensed mass of fibers ready for spinning.

satin weave—a basic weave characterized by loosely interlocked surfaces similar to irregular twills. This weave is rarely used by the handweaver.

secondary color—the product of two primary colors; orange, green, and violet.

selvage—the side, or edge, of a fabric.

sett—the number of warp threads per inch; the density of a fabric.

shag weave—any weave that uses a long, cut pile.

shed—an opening between warp threads through which the weft is passed.

shed stick, or shed sword—a flat, smooth stick used to produce a shed on a simple loom.

shot—see pick.

shuttle—the device that carries the weft, or filling, through the warp. The fingers substitute for the shuttle on a nail frame loom.

shuttle stick—a flat shuttle.

singles yarn—a yarn composed of only 1 strand.

slit—a vertical opening, especially in tapestry, created by weaving sections of the warp.

sword—a flat stick used to separate the warp threads and press the weft into the warp.

tabby—plain weave; also the binding thread between pattern picks in a pattern weave.

takeup—the extra thread allowed for lacing over and under the opposing set of threads; the warp becomes tighter as the weaving progresses, and the slack in the warp is taken up in the weaving.

tapestry—a weft-face, plain-weave fabric in which the weft is discontinuous.

tapestry comb, or tapestry fork—a tool that replaces the beater in tapestry weaving.

tension—the tightness or looseness of warp threads.

tension stick—a stick used to take up any slack in the warp and tighten the tension; used especially on a frame loom.

tertiary color—a color created by combining adjacent primary and secondary colors.

thread—in weaving terminology a synonym for yarn; sometimes refers to a tightly twisted yarn.

tubular double weave—a weave that forms two distinct layers of fabric connected at both selvages.

twill—a basic weaving construction characterized by diagonal lines.

twining—a construction in which 2 or more weft yarns are twisted around one another as they interlace with the warp.

unbalanced weave—a weave in which either the warp or the weft yarns are more concentrated; tapestry is an unbalanced, or **off-balanced,** weave.

value—the lightness or darkness of a color.

warp—the threads stretched lengthwise on the loom.

warp-face fabric—a fabric in which the warp threads dominate or cover the weft completely.

weave—the pattern, or order, in which the warp and weft are interlaced; it determines the construction.

weaving—the process by which any flexible material is interlaced at right angles to produce a surface; a series of taut, parallel, lengthwise, vertical threads—the warp—is interlaced with another series of mobile, horizontal, crosswise threads—the weft.

web—the part of the warp that is woven.

weft—threads crossing the width of the warp; also called **woof** or **filling.**

yarn—a continuous strand of material spun from natural or synthetic fibers or filaments.

INDEX